SAMUEL AND HIS GOD

Studies on Personalities of the Old Testament

James L. Crenshaw, Series Editor

SAMUEL AND HIS GOD

MARTI J. STEUSSY

The University of South Carolina Press

Published by the University of South Carolina Press
Columbia, South Carolina 29208

www.sc.edu/uscpress

Manufactured in the United States of America

19 18 17 16 15 14 13 12 11 10   10 9 8 7 6 5 4 3 2 1

Library of Congress Cataloging-in-Publication Data

Steussy, Marti J., 1955–
Samuel and his God / Marti J. Steussy.
p. cm. — (Studies on personalities of the Old Testament)
Includes bibliographical references and indexes.
ISBN 978-1-57003-924-9 (cloth : alk. paper)
1. Samuel (Biblical judge) 2. Bible. O.T. Samuel—Criticism, interpretation, etc. I. Title.
BS580.S2S74 2010
222'.406092—dc22

2010008117

This book was printed on Glatfelter Natures, a recycled paper with 30 percent postconsumer waste content.

CONTENTS

SERIES EDITOR'S PREFACE

Critical study of the Bible in its ancient Near Eastern setting has stimulated interest in the individuals who shaped the course of history and whom events singled out as tragic or heroic figures. Rolf Rendtorff's *Men of the Old Testament* (1968) focuses on the lives of important biblical figures as a means of illuminating history, particularly the sacred dimension that permeates Israel's convictions about its God. Fleming James's *Personalities of the Old Testament* (1939) addresses another issue, that of individuals who function as inspiration for their religious successors in the twentieth century. Studies restricting themselves to a single individual—e.g., Moses, Abraham, Samson, Elijah, David, Saul, Ruth, Jonah, Job, Jeremiah—enable scholars to deal with a host of questions: psychological, literary, theological, sociological, and historical. Some, like Gerhard von Rad's *Moses,* introduce a specific approach to interpreting the Bible, hence provide valuable pedagogic tools.

As a rule, these treatments of isolated figures have not reached the general public. Some were written by outsiders who lacked a knowledge of biblical criticism (Freud on Moses, Jung on Job) and whose conclusions, however provocative, remain problematic. Others were targeted for the guild of professional biblical critics (David Gunn on David and Saul, Phyllis Trible on Ruth, Terence Fretheim and Jonathan Magonet on Jonah). None has succeeded in capturing the imagination of the reading public in the way fictional works like Archibald MacLeish's *J. B.* and Joseph Heller's *God Knows* have done.

It could be argued that the general public would derive little benefit from learning more about the personalities of the Bible. Their conduct, often less then exemplary, reveals a flawed character, and their everyday concerns have nothing to do with our preoccupations from dawn to dusk. To be sure, some individuals transcend their own age, entering the gallery of classical literary figures from time immemorial. But only these rare achievers can justify specific treatments of them. Then why publish additional studies on biblical personalities?

The answer cannot be that we read about biblical figures to learn ancient history, even of the sacred kind, or to discover models for ethical action. But what remains? Perhaps the primary significance of biblical personages is the light they throw on the imaging of deity in biblical times. At the very least, the Bible constitutes human perceptions of deity's relationship with the world and its creatures. Close readings of biblical personalities therefore clarify ancient understandings of

God. That is the important datum which we seek—not because we endorse that specific view of deity, but because all such efforts to make sense of reality contribute something worthwhile to the endless quest for knowledge.

James L. Crenshaw
Duke Divinity School

ACKNOWLEDGMENTS

This book owes its existence to James L. Crenshaw. He taught me much of what I know about biblical scholarship and also specifically requested that my 1999 book, *David: Biblical Portraits of Power,* be followed by an additional volume on Samuel. Most of the writing took place during a research leave granted by the trustees of Christian Theological Seminary. I am grateful to them and to my faculty colleagues, who so capably sustained the school's teaching and administrative work in my absence. The Bibleworks 5.0 computer program (Bibleworks L.L.C., 2001) and my daughter Cally, who returned from Japan just in time to help with final critique and proofreading, have also greatly assisted my work.

I thank Jean Denton, Gordon Chastain, Linda Ferreira, Michael St. A. Miller, Mark Mousse, Antony Campbell, and my colleagues in the Network of Biblical Storytellers Scholars Seminar for conversations in which I worked out my thinking about the Samuel stories. I dedicate this book to my teachers and to my students, who perpetually refresh my vision of the Bible.

ABBREVIATIONS

BOOKS OF THE BIBLE

Old Testament

1 C	1 Chronicles	Jdg	Judges
2 C	2 Chronicles	1 K	1 Kings
Dt	Deuteronomy	2 K	2 Kings
Ex	Exodus	Lev	Leviticus
Ezek	Ezekiel	Mic	Micah
Gen	Genesis	Num	Numbers
Isa	Isaiah	Ps	Psalms
Jer	Jeremiah	1 S	1 Samuel
Josh	Joshua	2 S	2 Samuel

Apocrypha

Sir	Sirach (Ecclesiasticus)

New Testament

Heb	Hebrews
Lk	Luke
Mt	Matthew

BIBLE TRANSLATIONS

ASV	American Standard Version (1901)
KJV	King James Version (1611)
NIV	New International Version (1984)
NJB	New Jerusalem Bible (1985)
NKJ	New King James Version (1982)
NLT	New Living Translation (1996)
NRSV	New Revised Standard Version (1989)
RSV	Revised Standard Version (1952)
TNK	JPS Tanakh (1985)

SAMUEL IN THE BIBLE

1 SAMUEL

1	Samuel's birth story
2	Samuel's childhood and the sins of Eli's sons
3:1–4:1	Samuel is called and established as a prophet.
7:3–17	Samuel as judge
8	Israel's request for a king
9–11	Saul established as king
12	Samuel's "farewell speech"
13, 15	Samuel announces LORD's rejection of Saul.
16:1–3	Samuel anoints David.
19:18–24	Samuel receives David, stands over Saul's frenzied prophesying.
25:1	Death notice
28	Samuel's ghost speaks to Saul.

OUTSIDE 1 SAMUEL

1 C 6:28, 33	Genealogy
1 C 9:22	Samuel helps David establish the Levites' duties.
1 C 11:3	Samuel as predictor of David's anointing
1 C 26:28	Samuel as donor to the temple
1 C 29:29	Samuel as record keeper
1 C 35:18	Samuel as prophet
Ps 6:6	Moses, Aaron, and Samuel as intercessors
Jer 15	Moses and Samuel as intercessors
Acts 3:24	Samuel as prophet
Acts 13:20	Samuel as prophet
Heb 11:32	Samuel in a list of leaders
Sir 46:13–20	Summary of Samuel's career
1 Esdras 1:20–21	Samuel as prophet
2 Esdras 7:108	Samuel as intercessor

SAMUEL AND HIS GOD

CHAPTER 1

INTRODUCTION

The prophet Samuel's story is told mostly in the first sixteen chapters of the book of 1 Samuel. Beginning with Samuel's birth in the first chapter, 1 Samuel goes on to describe how Samuel grows up as servant to the priest Eli, whom he eventually replaces as the primary mediator between LORD[1] and Israel. Under Samuel's leadership the people of Israel—who at this point have no other formal leader—enjoy relief from foreign attackers. But when Samuel grows too old to lead the people himself, they ask him to appoint a king. LORD tells a reluctant Samuel to comply. Samuel anoints Saul, who has some promising early successes but eventually loses LORD's support. After Samuel has communicated this news to Saul, LORD sends Samuel to anoint David. The rest of 1 Samuel is primarily about David and Saul, with Samuel mentioned only a few times. He makes his final appearance as a ghost, summoned by Saul, who declares that on the morrow, "LORD will give Israel along with you into the hands of the Philistines" (1 S 28:19; this and all subsequent biblical quotations are from the New Revised Standard Version of the Bible, unless otherwise indicated).

I first paid serious attention to the biblical character Samuel when a student asked me to preach on 1 Samuel 3 at his ordination. The student, whose great passion was ministry with children, had chosen the chapter because in it LORD calls to the young Samuel as the boy sleeps in the temple. Since my student mostly wanted to show that even a very young person can be called by God, he trimmed the reading to leave out God's actual message to Samuel in 3:11–14, a message formulated to "make both ears of anyone who hears of it tingle" (3:11).

Now this student, who had been my teaching assistant, knew full well that I do not think problematic verses should be clipped from readings (as they so frequently are in church Bible lessons). If people have a problem with something in the Bible, I think they should talk about it rather than proclaiming respect for the Bible while censoring—if not downright misrepresenting—it. Furthermore, in my experience people grow far more by wrestling with difficult passages than by lingering over old favorites. The ordinand was, I am sure, not at all surprised when I began my sermon with the omitted verses, in which LORD says, "On that day I will fulfill against Eli all that I have spoken concerning his house, from beginning to end. For I have told him that I am about to punish his house forever, for the iniquity that he knew, because his sons were blaspheming God, and he did not restrain them. Therefore I swear to the house of Eli that the iniquity of Eli's house shall not be expiated by sacrifice or offering forever" (3:12–14).

It is not hard to see why these verses were left out. They are rather sobering from the standpoint of ministry to children. The target of LORD's condemnation, Eli, is not some stranger to Samuel. Eli is the person to whom Samuel's mother, Hannah, brought her child as soon as he was weaned, fulfilling an earlier vow that if she conceived she would dedicate her child to LORD (1 S 1). While his mother had reportedly visited him once a year, bringing a new robe for him each time (2:19), it was Eli who cared for and taught Samuel. Their closeness shows when Eli addresses Samuel as "my son" in 3:6 and 16. How does the young Samuel feel when he hears LORD's declaration of punishment against Eli? What is he thinking as he lies in the temple during the long hours after his visitation until dawn (3:15)? Is this really the story we want to use to teach children that God may have something to say to them?

In commentaries and preaching resources on the chapter, interpreters asserted Eli's corruption and the deservedness of LORD's punishment with a vehemence that looked for all the world like "protesting too much." For instance, a popular online commentary, David Guzik's *Enduring Word Media,* comments that LORD's word was rare (3:1) "probably, because of the hardness of heart among the people of Israel and the corruption of the priesthood. God will speak, and guide, when His people seek Him, and when His ministers seek to serve Him diligently." Guzik further tells us that being unable to see (3:2) "was true spiritually of Eli, as much as it was physically."

I concluded that perhaps I was not the only person unsettled by this oracle of punishment. I began to question it. Does Eli's dimming physical vision really symbolize spiritual blindness? Eli's physical eyes may not be able to see, but he can perceive who is calling Samuel and tell the clueless boy (who cannot tell the difference between LORD's voice and Eli's) how to reply (3:8). Meanwhile the supposed paragon of new faith, Samuel, fails to follow Eli's instructions: instead of answering, "Speak, LORD, for your servant is listening," as Eli advises, Samuel says simply, "Speak, for your servant is listening" (3:9–10). Possibly Samuel's dropping of LORD's name is an inconsequential variation, but I have learned from scholars such as Robert Alter (1981), Adele Berlin (1983), and Meir Sternberg (1985) to pay close attention to repetition in biblical narratives and ask if exact or inexact repetitions suggest some nuance of meaning. I wondered if the child Samuel actually doubted Eli's conclusion about the speaker and was hedging his bets by leaving out the divine name when he answered.

Then I noticed something even more disturbing. LORD says in 3:11 that Eli's "sons were blaspheming God, and he did not restrain them." But according to the previous chapter, Eli *did* make a spirited attempt to restrain his sons. They refused to listen, but the reason given is not that Eli has been lax in his exhortation. Rather we are told that "they would not listen to the voice of their father; for it was the will of the LORD to kill them" (2:23–25). LORD condemns Eli for the sons' failure to reform, but the narrative has already named LORD's intervention as their reason for persisting in sin. This is a God who is not merely harsh, but one who shifts blame for divine actions onto humans (Fokkelman 1993, 177).

Given this troublesome aspect of LORD's words, I did not rush to align myself with the divine condemnation of Eli. Instead I observed in the sermon that my student was shifting from the role of Samuel to that of Eli, and he might learn something from the virtues of the older character in the story. Eli keeps trying even when he does not get much support from above, has the perceptiveness and generosity to instruct his fosterling in responding to a voice that Eli himself cannot hear, and accepts LORD's bitter sentence without raging against the youngster who reports the message and who will take Eli's place. Would that more of us in teaching and ministry had the faithfulness and skill to send our charges so generously to places we ourselves cannot go! I noted, as comfort for those of us in roles more like Eli's than Samuel's, that while 1 Samuel 2–3 may leave the impression that all positive connections between Eli's family and LORD are being terminated, the cutoff is not absolute: the prophet Jeremiah seems to be a descendant of Eli.[2]

The preaching of this sermon piqued my curiosity about how people respond to Samuel. Most Bible readers are, in my experience, uneasy with him. This uneasiness arises in part from the negativity of Samuel's messages. From the oracle against Eli at the beginning of Samuel's career to the message of death that his ghost delivers the night before Saul's final battle ("Tomorrow you and your sons shall be with me; the LORD will also give the army of Israel into the hands of the Philistines"; 1 S 28:19), Samuel speaks stern warnings and predicts destruction. Worse yet (remember that oracle against Eli), it is not always obvious that the condemnations are deserved.

Even relatively inexperienced readers sense the problem. I ask students in my Introduction to the Old Testament class to write questions related to biblical readings, and one semester a striking twenty-six of twenty-eight students asked whether Samuel's condemnation of Saul in 1 Samuel 13 is fair (Steussy 2000, 126). In this story Saul, who has experienced some initial military successes, musters the Israelites at Gilgal (a site that the book of Joshua associates with the beginning of Israel's successful conquest of Canaan). This is the place were Saul's kingship has been confirmed and celebrated in 1 Samuel 11:14–15. The Philistines muster, too, with "thirty thousand chariots, and six thousand horsemen, and troops like the sand on the seashore in multitude" (13:5). The frightened Israelites hide in caves, cisterns, and even tombs; some flee to the other side of the Jordan (13:6–7). Now comes the crucial verse: Saul, we are told, "waited seven days, the time appointed by Samuel; but Samuel did not come to Gilgal, and the people began to slip away from Saul" (13:8).

The words, "the time appointed by Samuel," apparently refer to 1 Samuel 10:8, where Samuel tells Saul that "you shall go down to Gilgal ahead of me; then I will come down to you to present burnt offerings and offer sacrifices of well-being. Seven days you shall wait, until I come to you and show you what you shall do." Saul has now gone to Gilgal and has "waited seven days, the time appointed by Samuel," but Samuel has not arrived. With the Philistines mustering and his volunteer army beginning to desert, Saul goes ahead and makes prebattle offerings without Samuel, who, after all, has also told him to "do whatever you see fit to do, for God is with you" (1 S 10:7).

As soon as Saul does this, Samuel arrives, accuses him of foolishness and disobedience to LORD, and declares in 13:13–14 that LORD has appointed someone else ruler. While this information is surely upsetting to Saul, it does nothing to resolve the immediate problem. The new appointee will not be identified (and then only to his family and Samuel) until chapter 16. Meanwhile Saul still has to cope with demoralized Israelite soldiers and threatening Philistine armies.

Of the twenty-six students who asked about the fairness of the condemnation, twenty-three pronounced it justified, citing Samuel's statement that Saul has disobeyed LORD's commandment (13:13). But what commandment has Saul broken? The narrator has told us in so many words that Saul did wait "the time appointed by Samuel." It is *Samuel* who does not arrive according to plan. The question of what commandment Saul is supposed to have broken will arise again later, but suffice it here to say that the very need to explain what it is that Saul has done wrong—not to mention the variety of answers proposed to that question—demonstrates that the nature of his disobedience is not obvious. The students sensed this, and that was why so many of them asked whether Samuel was being fair. But they backed away from their own accurate perceptions, assuming that because Samuel is a prophet, he must therefore be right.

A number of scholars writing about Samuel and Saul have shown greater resistance to the idea that the prophet must always be right or at least must be expressing God's opinion. David Gunn in *The Fate of King Saul* presses the issue particularly hard. He points out that in 1 Samuel 8:6 the people's request for "a king to govern us" assigns the king a duty of governing (Hebrew *špṭ*—for more, see the section "Judge" in chapter 3) that has hitherto belonged to Samuel (mentioned four places in 1 Samuel 7) and that Samuel has tried to pass to his own sons (8:1). A king will thus replace Samuel and his sons. LORD's assurance to Samuel that "they have not rejected you" confirms that Samuel has complained about precisely such a rejection (8:7; Gunn 1980, 59). We cannot take Samuel's words about Saul as a transparent window onto LORD's viewpoint, because Samuel is not a disinterested broker between LORD and the king. Samuel has a stake in seeing Saul fail.

As further evidence of the possibility of disconnect between Samuel's viewpoint and LORD's with regard to kings, notice that after the people ask for a king, LORD tells Samuel three times (1 S 8:7, 9, and 22) to "listen to their voice" (a biblical idiom meaning "obey them") and anoint them a king. Instead Samuel says to them, "Each of you return home" (8:22). Lyle Eslinger comments that Samuel "has heard nothing Yahweh has said and seeks only to dissuade the people from their purpose" (1985, 271). Later, in 16:1 and 6–7, LORD openly chides Samuel for his attitudes about anointing Saul's replacement. Samuel's disgruntlement and obstructionism with respect to kingship well support Robert Alter's assessment: "The prophet Samuel may have God on his side, but he is also an implacable, irascible man, and often a palpably self-interested one as well" (1999, xv).

The fact that Samuel has his own agenda does not, as Alter recognized, preclude a close relationship between Samuel and LORD. If the dispute in 1 Samuel 13 is indeed over Samuel's instruction that Saul wait seven days for him (10:8), one might ask if such an instruction from Samuel really qualifies as "the commandment of the LORD your God, which he commanded you" (Samuel's phrasing in 13:13). LORD does not, however, disown responsibility for the command. Elsewhere Samuel tells the people, "The wickedness that you have done in the sight of the LORD is great in demanding a king for yourselves" (12:17). This evaluation squares with LORD's comment that "they have rejected me from being king over them" (8:7), but it sits less well with LORD's description of Saul as LORD's own chosen savior for the people (9:16). Given the conflicting evidence about LORD's attitude, it is an open question whether the indignation in 1 Samuel 12 originates with LORD (as Samuel seems to want the people to believe) or with the noticeably touchy Samuel. When Samuel prays for a thunderstorm, however, LORD sends one (12:17–18).

Each time I read 1 Samuel 12's account of Samuel praying for a thunderstorm and LORD delivering it, I recall the end of the calling-in-the-temple story. "As Samuel grew up, the LORD was with him and let none of his words fall to the ground. . . . And the word of Samuel came to all Israel" (3:19–4:1). What is odd about this is that I would expect Samuel not to let any of LORD's words fall to the ground (rather than the other way around), with the result that LORD's word (not Samuel's) would come to all Israel. It is almost as if LORD decides simply to back what Samuel says, which would be one way of understanding the thunderstorm incident.[3]

The closeness between Samuel and LORD may itself be a source of uneasiness as we read Samuel's story. Could we be troubled by a prophet who is close to LORD because there is something troubling about the way LORD is portrayed in these chapters? Most Jews and Christians have been taught that God is good, trustworthy, and wants people to treat one another with compassion, and most of us inject that conviction into our reading of Bible passages. If Bible stories contain material that contradicts those beliefs, we usually manage not to see it. (I have already mentioned how often Christian lectionaries trim offending verses out of their readings.) For instance, the conviction that God gives life and helps barren women is so pervasive that most readers celebrate Lord's giving of a child to Hannah in 1 Samuel 1 without ever noticing that Lord is said to be responsible for her barrenness to begin with. In 2:30–31 an anonymous "man of God" says to Eli on behalf of God, "I promised that your family . . . should go in and out before me forever; but now the Lord declares . . . I will cut off your strength and the strength of your ancestor's family." Many interpreters respond, as they do to 1 Samuel 3, by rehearsing justifications for the cutting-off, while avoiding the uncomfortable question of Lord's reliability. If Lord here recalls making a promise "forever" and nonetheless revokes it, what are the implications for other promises made by Lord?

When we reach the scene where "Samuel hewed Agag [the captured Amalekite king] in pieces before the Lord" (1 S 15:33), the violence is hard to overlook. It is, however, apparently what Lord wants (see 15:3). Indeed Saul is rejected precisely because he has "spared" Agag (15:9; the Hebrew word here could also be translated "showed compassion" or "had pity," as in 1 Samuel 23:21 and 2 Samuel 12:6). If Samuel is brutally violent in this scene, it is because he serves a lord who (at least according to this chapter) desires such behavior.

I have heard yet another kind of reaction to Samuel from students whose church traditions accord extremely high respect and authority to the pastor. A handful of such students have told me that Samuel reminds them of pastors they have known, sometimes their own mentors in ministry. These mentors were powerful, well-loved leaders who had earned respect by years of wise advice and courageous leadership. But eventually their leadership would be challenged, and the results could be ugly. The pastors seemed unable to accept that others might responsibly differ in their assessments of where the church should go. Too quickly, sometimes, the pastors equated questioning of their own programs with disobedience to God (compare Samuel's apparent reference to his own instruction as "the commandment of the Lord your God" in 13:13). Sometimes they used their power not only to resist but to punish those who, in their view, stepped out of line (compare the thunderstorm in 12:18). Always they were hurt and confused by what they perceived as the ungratefulness of their congregations (compare Samuel's "testify against me" in 12:3).

One student presented a drama, based on Samuel's farewell speech in 1 Samuel 12, in which such a pastor confronted his elders in a "come-to-Jesus meeting" about their support for an associate's new program. In 12:17–18, Samuel prays for a thunderstorm on the day of the wheat harvest, which might well mean loss of the entire year's crop. In the drama the pastor told the elders that he had prayed regarding their factory jobs and they should consequently expect to receive pink slips. You could feel his love for his church, conviction that he was following God's will, and disquiet at what he saw as the elders' mistakes. But the elders, too, had done much thinking and praying. They could not comprehend his failure to embrace new programs, and they were dismayed that he took their concerns as a total rejection of his, and God's, leadership. Although the pastor referred to the pink slips as an act of "tough love," to the elders it felt like rejection and to the audience it looked like personal retaliation.

What this student correctly perceived was that 1 Samuel 12, and the story of Samuel more generally, is not a simple tale of a good prophet setting a bad people straight about what God wants for them. It is a story about conflict over who should be in charge, played out not just in terms of ordinary human power, but in claims about God's intentions for the community. The student recognized real sincerity and possibly even some truth in Samuel's and the pastor's convictions that they were representing God's will. He recognized what a painful position such persons are in when they believe that God has asked them to lead in a certain direction and the community balks at following. But he also recognized that the spokesperson's own stake in the position creates a possibility of slippage. However sincere the person speaking for God, who guarantees that the speaker will not confuse his or her own agenda with God's?

Almost everyone can recognize that questions of this kind do turn up in contemporary religious life. Not everyone is as comfortable supposing that this may be the case with Samuel himself. "Does not the Bible show us that he was aligned with God?" a reader may legitimately ask.

To that I have two answers. First, it is generally true that Samuel and LORD are shown working as partners. However, as I have already shown and will later show in more detail, at points the 1 Samuel text itself gives us grounds to suspect divergences between Samuel's opinions and LORD's.

That method, however, takes the biblical narrator's (or narrators') account as the baseline for God's position. But who then tells this story? I suspect it is told by people who claim an authority similar to Samuel's, authority to instruct the people and their kings about what God wants and even to install or depose kings based on their obedience to that instruction. So my second answer is that because of the storytellers' probable stakes in depicting Samuel's closeness to God, we need to reckon with the possibility of slippage (however sincere) even in the narrators' account of God's position vis-à-vis Samuel.

In so saying, I reveal that I am not a historical or spiritual inerrantist. I do not believe that the Bible gives us divinely guaranteed historical information or even infallible spiritual guidance. My doubt about historical inerrancy comes not only from the discrepancies between biblical accounts and other sources of historical information, and not only from knowing how much the Bible resembles other ancient Near Eastern documents that we would never dream of regarding as entirely historically trustworthy, but above all from the internal evidence of the Bible itself. Its multiple accounts refuse to merge into a single smooth storyline, though the effort at merger has provided careers for many persons over the centuries. Even in the chapters that tell Samuel's story, not all the historical markers line up. I point out several such discrepancies in the course of this book.

I also do not consider the Bible spiritually infallible, and my reasons are empirical. There has been too much mischief and flat-out evil committed in its name for me to be able to say with a straight face that the Bible provides reliable guidance to anyone who sincerely seeks it. Others might reasonably reply that the problem is not with the Bible but with the depravity of those who interpret it. I might even agree with them, except that if a Bible intended to communicate God's message to humans is so easily corrupted by human interpretation, what sense does it make to call it infallible? As soon as we qualify infallibility with the requirement of correct interpretation, the game changes: we are no longer talking about the Bible as a simple, reliable source in which anybody can look up the right answers. Instead we are dealing with the competing authority claims of its interpreters. Granted, many of those interpreters deny that they are advancing their own authority. They claim that they are just following the rules set by the Bible itself. The trouble is, the same claim can be and often is made by other interpreters who arrive at different results. Even when we seek to be faithful to the Bible's own principles, human judgment plays an inescapable role in biblical interpretation.

While the track record of religious communities may prompt me to doubt the Bible's moral infallibility, it also testifies to the Bible's helpfulness and potential for good. Millions of people, many of them very simple in their faith (and others less simple), have found the Bible a source of hope, healing, wholeness, guidance, courage, and moral insight. The Bible has inspired lives that are admired well beyond the bounds of Judaism and Christianity.

I teach in an urban ecumenical seminary with students from a wide variety of Christian traditions and even occasionally from non-Christian traditions. Many come in assuming that the Bible presents plain truth that needs only to be embraced. Such views may have served them well in the past, but as our diverse community grapples with complex problems of racism, religious prejudice, sexual identity, and so forth, "simple" truths often turn out to be inadequate, or at least terribly complicated to apply. In this context an awareness of the Bible's complexity often turns out to be helpful. It can be useful to realize that the Bible does not offer just one set of answers and that its people struggled with problems discernibly like ours at many points. Understood in this way, the Bible helps us by illuminating the questions (as in the issues around Samuel's calling and Eli's displacement or the parallels between Samuel's farewell speech and a "come-to-Jesus meeting") rather than by giving us straightforward answers. It is in such a spirit that I pursue the exploration of Samuel.

The student who went to 1 Samuel 3 for a story about God's concern for children and the students who so desperately wanted Samuel's condemnation of Saul to be fair brought assumptions about God (and prophets, and the Bible itself) that were not well supported by the particular texts they were looking at. The students who interpreted Samuel in light of their own experiences with powerful religious leaders had a more serviceable matrix. Who is Samuel? Who is Lord? Is Samuel cantankerous because the people he serves are stubborn and ungrateful or because the lord he serves is so touchy and demanding? Or both, or neither? Is Lord's touchiness a divine fact, or do Samuel and the storytellers describe Lord as touchy because it fits with their own way of experiencing the world? How are these accounts of God colored by the dynamics of human personalities and struggles for religious power?

These questions lead us to ask who wrote 1 Samuel, and why, matters addressed in chapter 2 of this book. There I point out some of the tensions (points on which we seem to get conflicting information or attitudes) and uncertainties (places where information is simply missing or given but interpretable in multiple ways) in Samuel's story. I also discuss some of the more prominent compositional theories that have been proposed to explain the book's unevenness. I do not regard these theories as "assured results of modern scholarship." Some are fairly widely accepted; none are universally embraced; and vigorous debate continues. But learning about the theories will reveal some complicated issues in the stories themselves and indicates that the composers may have been responding to somewhat different questions than those we now ask.

Since our perception of Samuel is colored by our ideas about prophets (recall the students saying that since Samuel is a prophet, his accusations against Saul must be fair), chapter 3 examines the meanings of the word "prophet." How does Samuel fit these stereotypes, and in what ways does he challenge them? Since prophet is not the only role assigned to Samuel, the chapter also explores the roles of judge (as presented in the book of Judges) and priest. Once again the point is less to arrive at a definitive answer than to examine our own presuppositions and get a sense of the diversity of the biblical presentation.

An aspect of the Samuel stories that troubles or at least puzzles many readers is the characterization of Lord, to which we turn in chapter 4. Based on what Lord says and does in these stories, what is Lord's personality and what are Lord's goals?

How does Samuel fit into Lord's program, as these chapters of the Bible present it? Do our own presuppositions about God help or hinder us in understanding what is happening in these stories?

Chapters 2, 3, and 4 identify common presuppositions about the Bible, prophets, and God, and show that those presuppositions do not always match up with what we encounter in 1 Samuel. In the course of that work, some of the Samuel stories are looked at in detail. With presuppositions questioned and some details already examined, chapter 5 goes through the Samuel stories in order. Who is Samuel? Why does he do the things he does? How does he feel about them? Can we give a coherent account of his personality and motives?

Finally, in chapter 6 it is time to reflect on what this book says about Samuel and his God. Part of that reflection focuses on the ancient world and on what Samuel's story may tell us about the worldviews and agendas of its tellers. Part of it asks what these things mean for us. Does the story of Samuel give us answers for our own religious lives?

CHAPTER 2

SOURCES OF THE SAMUEL STORIES

"THE BIBLE"

Today we read stories about the prophet Samuel in the 1 Samuel subunit of a larger book we call "the Bible."[1] The fact that Samuel's story is biblical invokes a whole set of assumptions and expectations. For starters, although the English word "Bible" comes from the Greek phrase *ta biblia*, which means "the books" (plural), the English word "Bible" is singular. This, especially when reinforced (as it often is) with religious teachings about the Bible as a source of God's truth (singular), often leads to a conscious or unconscious assumption that the information and attitudes conveyed in different parts of the Bible will easily combine into a single unified outlook. Furthermore, today the Bible's primary function is religious. Therefore even people who do not accept the religious teachings of the Bible usually think of it as a book that presents such teaching, and they may very well assume that from the very outset the primary intention of its writers was to cultivate a particular understanding of and attitude toward God. Most of the Bible comes to us, however, from a time when the concept "Bible," as we know it or even as it would have been known at the beginning of the common era, had not yet developed. It would never have occurred to the earlier authors that they were writing "the Bible," because that idea did not exist in their world. Nor is the book they have bequeathed to us unified. Its very storyline contains contradictions, as when 1 Samuel 15:35 says that "Samuel did not see Saul again until the day of his death" but 19:22–24 tells of a later meeting between Samuel and Saul.

This chapter looks at some of the abundant evidence that has led scholars to posit a long history of development for 1 Samuel. I then introduce some widely accepted ideas about the layers of composition we encounter in the book. I want to be clear that these theories are speculative: we do not have copies of the proposed earlier editions of Samuel, except as they may be present in the finished book. I think we can be confident that its composition took place over several centuries and involved multiple people. I am less confident in particular theories about dates, purposes, and which verses should be assigned to which source.

If one believes, as I do, that interpretation should rest on what is present in the book now, why even discuss compositional history? The answer is that the variations in voice, characterization, and viewpoint discerned by historical-critical scholars *are* features of the present story. (Indeed source criticism was originally called "literary criticism" because of its close attention to matters of literary style.) One never reads without imagining some context for the communication, and trying to interpret discontinuities in Samuel's story as deliberate effects introduced by a single teller is no less speculative than supposing that we may be hearing different voices. For me, the concepts of a Saul story, a story of David's rise, a Prophetic Record, and a Deuteronomistic History conveniently capture relationships between various parts of Samuel's story and provide a helpful way of understanding their agendas. I believe that the relationships and agendas to which these terms point would continue to have interpretive significance even if the present ideas about composition were proven wrong.

After sketching some of the theories about compositional layers in the Samuel stories, I then discuss the challenge to historical-critical methods by scholars who use modern literary (not source) criticism to read the present story as a unified whole. These critics have paid very close attention to the nuances of the text, and I mention their work frequently herein. But their approach, too, has been challenged by scholars who believe that 1 and 2 Samuel, as we have them now, were never meant to be read as continuous stories. The chapter ends with a consideration of that challenge.

ANCIENT CUSTOMS OF AUTHORSHIP

Our tendency to assume unified authorship for biblical books is understandable not only in light of religious insistence on the Bible's unified truth but in light of writing customs in our own time. Most books today are the work of a single author presenting that author's viewpoint about the subject under discussion. The words of other authors will be identified with quotation marks or, if the book is a collection of essays by different authors, each chapter will bear the name of the person who wrote it. In a book published today, the text is almost always copyrighted, and legal action can be taken against anyone who misquotes it or uses it without attribution.

Part of the reason for modern protectiveness toward an author's exact words is that those words are potentially a money-making commodity. But in the ancient world, authors made no money from the sale of books. Most people could not read, and even for those who could, acquiring a scroll (or clay tablets, which were the preferred writing medium in some regions) meant either gaining possession of the original or commissioning a handmade copy. The materials were expensive and the project required many, many hours of work by a highly educated scribe, so a work did not get copied unless somebody valued it highly. The copies were not always exact, however. During the period in which the Hebrew Bible was composed, patrons and their scribes apparently felt free to revise and update the material being copied. Archaeologists have been able to trace similar processes for some compositions popular in Mesopotamia, uncovering different versions from different time periods showing that the material was gradually modified and added to over time.

Rough modern parallels might be the production of updated textbook editions in the sciences or the habit that most denominations have of periodically updating hymnals and worship books. In our world, however, we clearly mark new editions as such, and we painstakingly document the sources of insertions. In the ancient world, changes were simply made. No one seems to have felt that this was an insult to the previous authors. Indeed, in those cultures that attached an author's name to a work (a custom more characteristic of the Greek than the ancient Semitic world), disciples appear to have felt free to issue work in the name of their master, which probably involved some mix of desiring to honor him and desiring to clothe the new work in his authority.

The books of 1 and 2 Samuel (which I sometimes simply call "Samuel" because they were once a single Hebrew scroll) do not carry an author's name. Some readers do assume, from the names of these books, that Samuel wrote them. This is unlikely, however, since the prophet's death is reported in 1 Samuel 25:1, and no claim is made that the rest of the narrative was foreseen and recorded by him.[2] We can see the revising process at work when we compare the books of Samuel and 1 Chronicles 10–29. Both works cover the time period of Saul and David. At points their wording is virtually identical, but each also includes material missing in the other. Most scholars think that the Chronicles writer had access to something very like the present books of Samuel, from which he (we assume that this writer was a man) copied some stories verbatim, while omitting other parts that did not relate to his theme and adding some new material. It could also be that both Samuel and Chronicles are expanding on a shorter, earlier source. Both scenarios for the connections between Samuel and Chronicles involve a step in which changes or additions are made to an earlier source.

There are also significant differences between the Masoretic Text (the Hebrew version regularized by Jewish scholars in the early Middle Ages, abbreviated MT) of Samuel and the Greek version (a translation probably made a couple of centuries before the common era, although the extant manuscripts of it are more recent). The Hebrew text of the Dead Sea scrolls of Samuel is, interestingly, closer to the Greek tradition than to the MT.[3] The similarities and differences between these Samuel texts, like those between Samuel and Chronicles, could be accounted for in several ways. Perhaps the original version of Samuel looked more like the MT, and scribes in the line leading to the Dead Sea scrolls and the ancient Greek translation tampered with it. Alternatively the lineage represented by the ancient Greek translation and the Qumran scrolls might be more "original," with the MT resulting from tampering that took place sometime after the Greek translation was done. Many scholars suspect that both the MT and Greek/Qumran traditions contain revisions to a common predecessor text. The one thing we can be sure of is that modification did take place, and the modifiers did not leave us footnotes about who they were, what they changed, or when and why they did it.

Given what we know about ancient writing and copying practices, it is not safe to assume that all of 1 Samuel was authored by a single writer presenting a unified point of view. That does not mean we should rule out the possibility of reading it *as if* it were written by a single author. However, we also need to wrestle with the possibility that material that looks as though it is the product of insertions or different editorial hands may be exactly that. Let us examine, then, some features that scholars have seen as evidence of multiple authorship in 1 Samuel.

EVIDENCE OF LAYERS IN 1 SAMUEL: A FIRST GLANCE

My consideration of possible historical layers in the Samuel books begins by looking at what the books say about the first king, Saul, and at Samuel's and God's attitudes toward him. Just prior to the first encounter between Samuel and Saul, the narrator inserts this information: "Now the day before Saul came, the Lord had revealed to Samuel: 'Tomorrow about this time I will send to you a man from the land of Benjamin, and you shall anoint him to be ruler over my people Israel. He shall save my people from the hand of the Philistines; for I have seen the suffering of my people, because their outcry has come to me.' When Samuel saw Saul, the Lord told him, 'Here is the man of whom I spoke to you. He it is who shall rule over my people'" (1 S 9:15–17). Samuel accordingly anoints Saul the next morning, saying, "The Lord has anointed you ruler over his people Israel. You shall reign over the people of the Lord and you will save them from the hand of their enemies all around" (1 S 10:1).

In these passages kingship is presented as God's plan, and Saul is God's chosen deliverer for the people. This theme continues in chapter 11, where the spirit of God comes upon Saul "with power" (11:6) and he leads the people in a triumphant confrontation with the arrogant and oppressive Ammonite king, Nahash. Thereupon "Samuel said to the people, 'Come, let us go to Gilgal and there renew the kingship.' So all the people went to Gilgal, and there they made Saul king before the Lord in Gilgal. There they sacrificed offerings of well-being before the Lord, and there Saul and all the Israelites rejoiced greatly" (1 S 11:14–15). First Samuel 14:47–48 summarizes Saul's reign this way: "When Saul had taken the kingship over Israel, he fought against all his enemies on every side—against Moab, against the Ammonites, against Edom, against the kings of Zobah, and against the Philistines; wherever he turned he routed them. He did valiantly, and struck down the Amalekites, and rescued Israel out of the hands of those who plundered them."

Presented with only this material, we would easily conclude that Saul was God's chosen leader for the deliverance of Israel and that he successfully carried out that task, with Samuel's endorsement. But just before the positive summary of Saul's kingship just quoted, Saul has been presented as at best indecisive and at worst downright incompetent, fumbling the opportunity presented by his son's daring victory over a Philistine garrison and ending up in a mere standoff with the enemy. In the early part of chapter 14, Saul asks the priest Ahijah to "bring the ark of God" (presumably to request an oracle) but then tells the priest, to "withdraw your hand" (14:18–19). He enjoins the troops to fast and then permits them to slaughter captured livestock to eat (14:24 and 34). He says the Israelites will "go down after the Philistines by night" to follow up on the day's victory but then decides to ask for an oracle first (14:36–37), and finally he swears that his son Jonathan must die but is talked out of it by the troops (14:44–46). These stories build toward the later accounts of his conflicted behavior with David. In 16:21, after David plays the lyre, "Saul loved him greatly, and he [David] became his armor-bearer," but in 17:55 Saul does not know who David is and in 18:11 and 19:10 he throws his spear at David. In 24:20 Saul acknowledges that David is destined to receive the throne and asks only an oath that David will not destroy Saul's descendants, but in 1 Samuel 26 he is again chasing David through the wilderness, then again calling David "my son" and blessing him.

Of course one can—and many do—explain this as psychological deterioration over time. But if Saul is really so unbalanced, why do the Israelites continue to follow him? Samuel has ceased to support him, we hear of no administrative apparatus by which Saul can coerce obedience, and David and Jonathan are both available as alternatives. The Israelites' continued loyalty to Saul sits uneasily with what we are asked to believe about his behavior.

Scholars make their living by disagreeing with one another and coming up with new theories, so of course they do not all agree on how to account for these different pictures of Saul, but most agree that we are seeing material from multiple storytellers. Many of the stories may come from close to the time of the events about which we are being told. A piece of evidence pointing in this direction would be the term *pîm*, mentioned as the price of sharpening a plowshare in the Hebrew text of 1 Samuel 13:21. This coin weight is not mentioned elsewhere in the Bible, so the term probably marks the story as fairly old. In 9:9, by contrast, we hear the comment that "formerly in Israel, anyone who went to inquire of God would say, 'Come, let us go to the seer'; for the one who is now called a prophet was formerly called a seer." Only a storyteller or editor from a later time would use "formerly" in this way.

I will not attempt to explain every theory about the composition of the books of Samuel; that has been done elsewhere.[4] It is common, however, for scholars to suppose that positive accounts of Saul, such as those found in 1 Samuel 9 and 11, originated with supporters who remembered him as successful. However, these accounts are now embedded in a narrative that portrays Saul as a ditherer or downright madman. That story, often referred to as the History of David's Rise, would have included such incidents as Saul's need for soothing in 1 Samuel 16:14–23, his jealousy in 18:6–8 (and elsewhere), and his recognition of David's legitimacy in 1 Samuel 26. It was quite possibly compiled by the spin doctors of David's court in order to counter rumors that David had schemed against and betrayed Saul (McCarter 1980b).

If these speculations are correct, then the earliest strata of 1 Samuel were composed not for religious instruction but to make particular leaders look good. Lord's support (or lack thereof) is emphasized because people believed that a divinely favored king would win battles and his nation would prosper agriculturally and economically. (See Psalm 72 for a strong statement of the hopes surrounding a God-backed king.) At best you would want to support Lord's chosen king because of all the collateral benefits that Lord's favor would provide for the king's subjects. At the very least, the king's propagandists would hope, military and political enemies would hesitate to attack a king who had strong divine backing.

It is perhaps natural that today's readers focus less on the political merits of Saul and David than on topics still debated in our own time, such as the character of God. But we are then asking a different question than did the authors, whose presentation of God seems limited, at times, to something like "God likes David, so you better line up with David" or "Prophets have the inside line to God, so you better listen to the prophets."

THE DEUTERONOMISTIC HISTORY

The merits of Saul are not the only issue on which 1 Samuel gives us conflicting information. The book also gives us a mixed report on whether kings are desirable at all. Contrast Samuel's and God's support for kingship in the material quoted earlier with their attitudes in the following passage: "The thing displeased Samuel when they said, 'Give us a king to govern us.' Samuel prayed to the Lord, and the Lord said to Samuel, '. . . They have rejected me from being king over them'" (1 S 8:6–7). And similarly in this passage: "In that day you will cry out because of your king, whom you have chosen for yourselves; but the Lord will not answer you in that day" (1 S 8:18). And yet again, Samuel's statement, in a speech following close upon the joyful king making reported in 11:14–15: "The wickedness that you [the people] have done in the sight of the Lord is great in demanding a king for yourselves" (12:18).

What connection do these passages have with the quite positive words from God reported in 1 Samuel 9:15–17? In 1943 the German scholar Martin Noth proposed that the Samuel books were part of a greater historical work stretching from Joshua through Judges and 1 and 2 Samuel to 1 and 2 Kings. (This work would not have included Ruth, which sits in a different section of the Jewish canon than the other books named here.) This work was, he thought, compiled after the fall of Jerusalem to highlight aspects of the people's history that explained the ultimate fates of Israel (the northern kingdom, which fell to Assyria in 721/722 B.C.E.) and Judah (the southern kingdom, ruled by David's descendants in Jerusalem until Babylon captured the city in 587/586 B.C.E.). Noth called this grand historical work "Deuteronomistic" because it drew upon the principles of the book of Deuteronomy, especially that work's demand for worship of LORD alone in a single centralized location, to explain why Israel and Judah fell.

Noth did not picture the Deuteronomistic compiler writing the whole story from scratch but assumed that the story drew upon and incorporated large chunks of older material. Noth attributed the bulk of 1 Samuel to pro-Saul and pro-David sources of the type we have already considered. But Noth proposed that the Deuteronomist made some crucial additions to this story, most notably the ardently antikingship speech in which Samuel describes the people's request for a king as a great "wickedness" (12:18). Noth saw this speech (along with similar ones in Joshua 1 and 23 and 1 Kings 8) as a key expression of the Deuteronomist's theology of history (1981, 5–6). In his view the bitter tone of Samuel's words in 1 Samuel 12 comes from the fact that the author is not Samuel, but the Deuteronomist, who writes after the nation and its kings have indeed been "swept away" (1 S 12:25). The Deuteronomist attributes Jerusalem's fall to the refusal of both the people and their kings, not just in Samuel's time but subsequently, to offer the obedience called for in the speech.

Noth's idea that the books from Joshua to 2 Kings are a unified narrative rather than an accidental series of independent books has found wide (although not universal) acceptance. His attribution of the work to a single exilic author, however, has received considerable challenge. Early on, Gerhard von Rad (1966, original publication 1947) noted that the optimism of some "Deuteronomistically" flavored passages makes it hard to understand them as mere postmortems for Israelite kingship. If kingship totally violates God's will and the kingdoms are doomed to destruction from the start, why does the history so stress God's election of, favor for, and promises to David? Especially striking are the reports of a reform conducted by King Josiah, near the end of Judah's national life, on exactly the lines favored by the Deuteronomist:

> The king [Josiah] went up to the house of the LORD, and with him went all the people of Judah, all the inhabitants of Jerusalem, the priests, the prophets, and all the people, both small and great; he read in their hearing all the words

> of the book of the covenant that had been found in the house of the LORD. The king stood by the pillar and made a covenant before the LORD, to follow the LORD, keeping his commandments, his decrees, and his statutes, with all his heart and all his soul, to perform the words of this covenant that were written in this book. All the people joined in the covenant. (2 K 23:2–3)

What more could even Samuel have asked for?

Following the covenant making just described, the reformer king Josiah destroys all idolatrous worship materials and places, and he orders a Passover celebration "as prescribed in this book of the covenant," such as had not "been kept since all the days of the judges who judged Israel" (2 K 23:21–22). Of Josiah it is said in the history, "Before him there was no king like him, who turned to the LORD with all his heart, with all his soul, and with all his might, according to all the law of Moses; nor did any like him arise after him" (2 K 23:25; compare Dt 6:5). How could this assessment have been offered by a historian who considered kingship a complete mistake and knew that the entire edifice had come crashing down not long after Josiah's early death?

Frank Moore Cross (1973, 274–89) responded to these questions with a proposal that the original version of the Deuteronomistic history was produced in conjunction with and support for Josiah's reformation, a few decades before Jerusalem's fall. This would account for the repeated mention of God's favor in David and promises of loyalty to David's descendants (of whom Josiah was one). In Cross's view the calls for obedience in the history's speeches are addressed in the first instance to a nation that can still hope God will keep those promises and support the monarchy. Cross suggests that only relatively minor updates and revisions (including 1 S 12:25: "but if you still do wickedly, you shall be swept away, both you and your king") were added by a later exilic editor, who touched up the history in light of the reform's failure and the fall of Judah.

How might thinking in terms of a Deuteronomistic History influence our reading of 1 Samuel? First, the Deuteronomistic theme of obedience to the "law of the LORD" is compatible with modern religious expectations, although even here, if Cross's suggestions are correct, the writers are supporting their king's efforts to centralize religious power in his own capital city, a motive we might today call political rather than religious. Noth and his later nuancers also call attention to the ways in which the Samuel stories relate to the larger history from Joshua to 2 Kings (in which context we now read them, regardless of the correctness of various compositional theories). How is our reading colored by knowing that the monarchy established in Samuel's time will split within a couple of generations and collapse entirely within a few hundred years? How do theologically programmatic sections like 1 Samuel 12 influence our understanding of the older stories about Saul and David? Meanwhile the older materials have not lost their voices. To interpret this multivoiced text faithfully, we have to honor its complexity.

THE PROPHETIC RECORD

Although the broad concept of a Deuteronomistic History has been widely accepted, discussion continues about the possible layers involved, with some scholars claiming evidence of multiple postexilic editorial passes and others attempting to refine our understanding of the material's preexilic compositional history. Most important for this book are proposals that between the propaganda narratives of the early monarchy and the first edition of the Deuteronomistic History stands a middle compositional layer dominated by northern, prophetically oriented (rather than Judean, Davidic-oriented) assumptions and interests. Important versions of this proposal have been presented by P. Kyle McCarter Jr. (1980a, 18–23) and Antony F. Campbell (1986; also explicated in Campbell and O'Brien 2000). McCarter and Campbell both believe that editors of a prophetic middle layer added bits to Samuel's story, such as the references to his early presence before Lord (1 S 2:18–21 and 26), that would have enhanced his image and underscored his authority to install and depose kings. Both believe that 1 Samuel 9 originally told of Saul's encounter with an anonymous seer who merely predicted that Saul would become king. It would have been the prophetic editors who identified that seer as Samuel and showed him actually anointing Saul. To these editors we would also owe the scene in which Samuel anoints David (1 S 16:1–13).

McCarter and Campbell differ over questions of dating and how much of the present 1 Samuel would have been included in a prophetic document. McCarter envisions prophetic editors working "during or shortly after the collapse of the northern kingdom" (22) near the end of the 700s B.C.E., when there would be good reason to be pessimistic about monarchy (although perhaps still reason to hope in the solidity of the Judean dynasty). His "Prophetic History" contains nearly all of 1 Samuel, even parts, such as 1 Samuel 12 (or the core thereof), that many scholars have seen as Deuteronomistic. McCarter indeed describes his hypothesized Prophetic History as "proto-Deuteronomic" (22). Campbell, by contrast, proposes a Prophetic Record compiled by persons associated with the prophet Elisha in the 800s B.C.E. It would not have included 1 Samuel 4–8, much of 10, and 12–14. Since these passages contain some of 1 Samuel's strongest antikingship statements, Campbell's proposed document is less critical of kingship than McCarter's. For Campbell's prophetic compilers, the issue would be not that kingship is itself wrong, but that prophets should have a determining voice with regard to who will be king and what that king will do.

The details of these competing proposals are uncertain enough that I would not wish to make my interpretation of Samuel absolutely dependent on either of them.

I do think, however, that McCarter and Campbell are right in supposing that the stories of Samuel have been significantly shaped by someone who has a strong stake in the authority of prophets vis-à-vis kings.

Beyond that, I am inclined to favor Campbell's proposal because I see in Samuel a prophet whose authority derives primarily from immediate knowledge of God's will. This idea of immediate prophetic authority fits closely with that expressed in the stories of anointings by Elijah and Elisha, to whose followers Campbell attributes his Prophetic Record.[5] McCarter's proposed prophetic compilers stand much closer to Deuteronomy proper.[6] For them, the prophet par excellence would be Moses, who delivers not just verbal instructions for his own generation, but the written regulations that form the core of Deuteronomy and are binding for all subsequent generations. While Samuel does seem much like Moses in some aspects of the finished story (note especially his writing of the "rights and duties of kingship" in 1 Samuel 10:25), I am inclined to agree with Campbell that these are later adjustments to a text that at its core emphasizes a more immediate prophetic authority.

TOO MUCH ANALYSIS OF LAYERS?

In the past half-century, many scholars have rebelled against the historical-critical quest to uncover the compositional and editorial histories of biblical books. The rebels accuse source critics, as well as redaction critics (who focus on the work of biblical editors), of directing their interpretive energy to hypothetical earlier documents (that may or may not have existed in the forms we imagine) at the expense of interpreting the biblical texts we actually have.

The rebels also accuse historical critics of holding too narrow an idea about what kinds of literature may have existed in the ancient world. Historical critics, they say, have assumed that each ancient source would have championed one simple cause, such as Saul's kingship, David's kingship, prophetic authority, or Josiah's reform. But the questions involved—for instance, whether kingship for Israel was a good idea—are not simple ones and obviously not ones on which everyone agreed. Why, ask the rebels, can we not imagine that the ancient writers would have produced materials that pondered complicated questions from multiple angles and probed a variety of possible answers to the questions? And furthermore, they ask, even if a process has occurred in which later editors have drawn together diverse source materials, why assume that we can make sense of their work only by breaking it down into component parts? Why not suppose that the resulting composition has its own artistry and logic, that the varying viewpoints have been brought together to produce some deliberate effect? After all, the finest literature of our own world is not monotone propaganda. Our greatest literature presents issues in ways that challenge simple answers and force us to ponder complex possibilities for making sense of them. Should we not at least ask whether tensions and apparent contradictions in biblical books might be deliberate and meaningful rather than a display of incoherence?

The books of Samuel have attracted much attention from these new critics, who often term their own method "literary" or "rhetorical." Robert Alter, one of the instigators of the new movement, deals extensively with the books of Samuel in his 1981 book *The Art of Biblical Narrative* (which is, by the way, an excellent introduction to this approach). He treats the Samuel books in even more detail in *The David Story* (1999), a translation that makes many literary nuances of the Hebrew text evident in English and also offers some trenchant commentary. Meir Sternberg's *Poetics of Biblical Narrative* (1985) explores many individual stories from the books of Samuel. J. P. Fokkelman's *Crossing Fates* (1993) and *Vow and Desire* (1986) cover the first parts of 1 Samuel in exhaustive detail, with particular attention to the patterning of motifs and a strong emphasis on psychological interpretation. Robert Polzin's *Samuel and the Deuteronomist* (1989), by contrast, probes literary resonances from the point of view of their possible meanings for exilic readers deeply concerned about how to interpret the fall of the monarchy.

Most of these interpreters do not in principle deny the possibility that biblical authors drew upon earlier sources, but in practice they hold that the most productive interpretive approach is one that looks for sense—not necessarily simple sense—in the "final form." But which final form, given that for the books of Samuel the Greek and Hebrew textual traditions vary noticeably? Most of these literary interpreters follow the Hebrew text. At points of blatant disruption they may look to the Greek/Qumran tradition for a more correct reading, but generally they do so less often than do standard translations such as the NRSV or NIV. While literary readers are not primarily interested in discerning earlier forms, they are quite aware of the textual discontinuities noted by more traditional historical-critical scholars.

Before I comment further on the current trend toward literary readings of biblical texts, it is worth noting that religious interpreters over the last two millennia have not been blind to the roughness of the text. Noting that Shiloh is said to have a "temple" (1 S 1:9 and 3:3), a claim that is in discord with the tradition that there was no temple before Solomon's, Theodore of Mopsuestia tells us that the tabernacle could be called a temple. Augustine, pointing to the tension between Lord's repentance (15:11 and 25) and Samuel's statement that Lord does not repent (15:29), says that "even though God said, 'I repent,' it is not to be taken according to the human sense" (Franke and Oden 2005, 210 and 255). Augustine's nonliteral reading lets him make sense of an apparent contradiction.

In recent centuries, particularly in Protestant traditions, there has been a shift in emphasis toward "plain meaning." But making coherent sense of the Bible's plain meaning can require as much creativity as figurative reading methods. A first reading of the Hebrew text of 1 Samuel 13:1 yields, "Saul was a year old when he began to reign; and he reigned two years over Israel." That does not make good sense, and even scholars who are reluctant to admit problems with the Hebrew text usually conclude that, in this case, something must have been miscopied. (The sentence is simply missing in the ancient Greek translation, so that does not help us reconstruct anything.) Rather than speculate about the missing information, the NRSV translators give us, "Saul was . . . years old when he began to reign; and he reigned . . . and two years over Israel," with footnotes indicating that numbers must have fallen out at the points indicated by the ellipses. NIV supplies "thirty" for the age of accession, with a footnote that this number is given by some late Greek manuscripts, and it inserts a "forty" before "two" in the length of reign, with a footnote telling us it has drawn this information from Acts 13:21. As a fairly extreme example of the kind of maneuver some commentators use to avoid admitting that the text contains errors, we can offer David Toshio Tsumura's translation: "A certain year of age was Saul when he became king, and just for two years he ruled over Israel" (2007, 330). Tsumura admits that the material about Saul suggests that his reign lasted a great deal longer than two years, but explains, "the expression *just for two years* is probably given from the author's, hence God's point of view: Saul was king only for 'two years,' even though he remained 'king' much longer in human eyes" (333, Tsumura's italics). I find it easier to believe—as have most other interpreters, even quite conservative ones, over the centuries—that either the information about Saul's reign was deliberately suppressed (perhaps by someone who found it awkward that a king allegedly so unacceptable to God enjoyed a long reign) or a copyist simply made a mistake here. I am more inclined toward the latter idea, especially in light of the fact that the books of Samuel contain many other verses where a copyist's eye seems to have skipped ahead, resulting in something being omitted from the text.[7]

At first glance the new wave literary interpreters are engaged in something quite different than traditional efforts to derive a straightforward and consistent viewpoint from the text. They are well aware of apparent unevennesses and generally deal with them by asserting that the tension is deliberate, rather than by straining to translate or explain theologically in a way that removes the tension. As an example, consider 1 Samuel 6:19. Chapters 4–6 have already told us how the ark of the covenant was captured by the Philistines, who put it in the temple of their god Dagon (presumably to show that Israel's god was a servant to Dagon). But then they find Dagon's statue on the floor, broken by no known human agency, and the inhabitants of the city are afflicted by panic and illness (seen in that era as signs of divine displeasure). Disruptions continue as the Philistines shuffle the ark from city to city. Finally the ark returns to Israelite territory by completely improbable means: two freshened dairy cows pull it straight uphill to its destination, although neither has ever been yoked to a cart before and their calves are still lowing in the barn behind them. This persuades the Philistine lords that a divine hand is at work. The people of Beth-Shemesh greet the ark's arrival in their town with rejoicing, burnt offerings, and sacrifices. The ark itself is handled by properly qualified Levites (1 S 6:13–15).

What happens next comes as something of a surprise. The Hebrew text says, "And he struck some of the people of Beth-shemesh, because they looked into the Ark of the Lord; and he killed seventy men, fifty thousand men. The people mourned because the Lord had made a great slaughter among the people" (1 S 6:19, following NRSV's notes).

Our first complication is that the Greek text reads rather differently: "The descendants of Jeconiah did not rejoice with the people of Beth-shemesh when they greeted the ark of the Lord; and he killed seventy men of them. The people mourned because the Lord had made a great slaughter among the people" (1 S 6:19, main NRSV text, which here follows the Greek). Whether the victims are "descendants of Jeconiah" or simply "some of the people of Beth-shemesh," and whether the victims number 70 (itself a significant number in an ancient city) or 50,070, the violence here is unexpected and the reasons for it unclear.

NRSV's alternate translation follows traditional interpretation when it says the offenders "looked into" the ark, an action that might be seen as violating divine boundaries enough to justify what happens next. Online commentator David Guzik clearly assumes such inappropriate looking when he comments, "There are things, because of the honor and glory of God, which He has chosen to keep hidden, and it is wrong for men to pry into these secrets of God" (www.enduringword.com).

But the Hebrew term used here (the verb *r'h,* meaning "see" or "look," followed by the preposition *b*) is not normally translated "looked into." This verb plus the preposition *b* normally denotes the simple act of "looking at" something (Hannah uses the same expression in 1:11 when she asks Lord to "look on" her misery). Literary reader Lyle M. Eslinger accordingly translates it, "because they looked at the ark" (1985, 218 and 453–454n10). In his view the comment about looking at the ark seems at first to offer a mitigating circumstance for the slaughter but in the end fails to justify it; it is an "ironic" mitigation. Eslinger says,

> Yahweh's response is made to appear totally incomprehensible by the narrator. It is as though Yahweh assaults the Bethshemeshites for simply looking at the ark. . . . Both before (ch. 4) and after the new exodus of the ark they suffer at his hands for no just cause. The rationale for Yahweh's actions is now hidden not only from the people in the narrative, as seemed to be the case for some

> in Ch. 4 (e.g. 4.3). The irony of the mitigation is shared by the omniscient narrator with his reader, who is now numbered among those who do not see the purpose of Yahweh. (220)

What a contrast to Guzik's explanation, which never considers the possibility that the slaughter is simply unjust. For Guzik, presumably, any action the Bible attributes to God must by definition be just.

The passage I have quoted from Eslinger's work illustrates two features found in the work of many literary critics. They are willing, first, to point out problematic and/or contradictory features of the text and, second, to ask if we are *supposed* to find these features problematic (as opposed to many traditional readers who assume that we are supposed to approve of everything God does in the Bible). At the same time Eslinger seems a bit overconfident when he tells us that the "reader. . . . is now numbered among those who do not see the purpose of Yahweh" (220). After all many, many generations of readers have failed to conclude that God smites the Beth-shemeshites "for no just cause." David Jobling, noting Eslinger's (and others') emphasis on the "omniscient narrator," comments, "By this they mean that the narrator *claims* omniscience, for example claims to know the secret thoughts of the characters, including God. But this quickly shades over into saying that the reader is obliged to accept the narrator's claim. . . . In this view interpretation is nothing more than discovering and following the indications the narrator skillfully provides, and it is bad interpretation to move outside this framework. This is not an omniscient, but an omnipotent narrator!" (1998, 142, Jobling's italics).[8] I would add, and I think Jobling would not disagree, that the diverse interpretations offered by literary critics suggest that the narrator's control is less determinative than they assert. As I noted earlier, religious commentary on scripture frequently appeals to the authority of the text when the real authority is the commenting author's own theological framework. In the same way, literary critics speak enthusiastically of the signals that the narrator uses to "control" our reading of the text, but at some point one needs to ask whether that control is actually coming from the biblical narrator or from the method of the commentator.

My own training focused on literary methods for reading the Bible. I highly value such methods' emphasis on the present text, willingness to see what is objectionable or of questionable coherence, and willingness to ask whether biblical writers might have intended something complicated. I quote the observations and interpretations of the literary commentators mentioned here, and others of similar persuasion, at many points in this book. I agree with Jobling, however, that biblical interpretation is an open-ended business and that we should be suspicious of *any* interpretation that claims to offer a single true reading.

WAS IT EVER MEANT TO BE READ ALL AT ONCE?

Some scholars attribute 1 Samuel's roughness to the presence of diverse, even incompatible sources, while others emphasize its unity and seek artistic purpose in its discontinuities. But even the source and redaction critics who most emphasize the bumpiness of the present book usually suppose that its final editors meant it to be read straight through. We need to consider another possibility. Could it be that the final editors did not intend for us to read 1 Samuel as a single continuous story? This view is offered by Antony F. Campbell and Mark A. O'Brien in a source- and redaction-critical work, *Unfolding the Deuteronomistic History.* In this book Campbell and O'Brien note that "editors and revisers who have worked on the canonical biblical texts have as a rule been intelligent people and . . . it is always rewarding to ponder the impact of their editing and revising. However, the caution remains that not all editing and revising needs to be aimed at producing a coherent text. There is a place for storage, for variants, for contrast and contradiction" (4). They explicitly reject the dogma "that the present narrative can be read as presenting a story's performance, the telling of the story. It is our conviction that much of the Bible's narrative text may contain reported stories, sketches of stories, summarized from stories already told and available for the telling of stories again; variants and other views can be noted in such reports" (7).

These authors believe that the compilers of the present written document gathered diverse materials for purposes of preserving and even cataloging them in an accessible order, but without attempting to synthesize or integrate them all (8). Their theory draws on a great deal of evidence that in the ancient world stories were always—even when being read from a scroll—told aloud. Furthermore ancient writing was so difficult to read (ancient Hebrew lacked vowels, punctuation, and capital letters) that probably no one would have attempted to read aloud without careful preparation beforehand. Campbell and O'Brien claim, however, that the Deuteronomistic History was not meant to be read aloud as written at all. Instead the teller would use the scroll as a source of ideas, some that he or she would use and some that the teller would skip over. So, for instance, a teller might use the court-musician version of David's arrival in Saul's court (1 S 16) or the Goliath-killing version of the meeting of David and Saul (1S 17), but not *both* in the same telling.

The Campbell/O'Brien understanding would explain why we get multiple versions of Saul's appointment as king (anointed by Samuel in 1 Samuel 10:1, chosen by the casting of lots and proclaimed to the assembly as king in 10:20–24, and made king again in 11:15), two versions of his repudiation by Samuel (13:13–14 and 15:22–23), and two accounts of the origin of the phrase "is Saul, too, among the prophets?" (1 S 10:1–12, 19:23–24). It is not that the editors did not notice the repetitions and occasional contradictions, say Campbell and O'Brien. Rather it is precisely because the differences were significant that the editors felt obliged to include multiple accounts, in order that valuable traditions not be lost. In this view what the final editors have given us is not a synthetic, integrated, single view of events, but a collection of competing accounts about how things happened. If this theory is true, then readers, including recent literary critics, who attempt to read the compendium as a sophisticated literary unity are working at cross-purposes to its creators' intent. It may be a sophisticated work, but it is a work of collection and preservation rather than integration.

We are faced here with two separate questions. The first question is historical: what, in our best judgment, were the intentions of the ancient writers and/or editors? Are we even supposed to be able to find an integrated meaning? With respect to this question, I believe that the literary critics are correct in arguing that we should not reject the possibility of a sophisticated unified artistry until we have at least attempted to find it. On this point, then, we must suspend judgment until we have assessed the proposals for finding a coherent overall reading of the narratives involving the prophet Samuel. I do note by way of anticipation, however, that at some points (for instance, the closing statements in 1 Samuel 7 that there was peace for all of Samuel's days, which are followed by many chapters describing anything but peace) I think we must conclude that we are faced with competing traditions.

The second question is practical. Whether or not the ancient editors intended to offer a single continuous story, their work comes to us via a tradition that expects to read it as a unified story. We can never know for sure what the ancient producers intended. Even if we knew what they intended, we could not reproduce that reading experience, because we live in a different world, bring different experiences to the reading, and cannot unlearn the intervening history. We live, for instance, in a world that has produced and explored political options unknown when the text of Samuel was assembled. We live also in a cosmopolitan, multicultural world where the negative consequences of claiming to have the single right answer are all too evident (or, at least, evident when someone else makes such a claim).

Since we cannot simply read as the ancients would have, how will we read for our own time? Will we find a unified sense in the story we have received or a more complex composite meaning? Or will we simply dissect it into components? I do my best, especially in chapters 4 and 5, which present sequential readings, to offer an understanding of Samuel's story as a whole. But I hope that the present chapter helps readers to understand why at some points I believe that honesty requires that we leave competing assertions unresolved. At such points my approach is closer to Campbell and O'Brien's than to that of the literary critics, as I propose that we imagine hearing our story told by several different tellers whose viewpoints do not quite coincide.

CHAPTER 3

THE MANY ROLES OF SAMUEL

In previous chapters I have referred to Samuel as a "prophet." However, this word is used only sparingly for him in the book of 1 Samuel itself. First Samuel 3:20 tells us that "all Israel from Dan to Beer-sheba knew that Samuel was a trustworthy prophet of the LORD." First Samuel 9 refers to him as a "seer," with an explanatory note in 9:9 that "seer" is an older word for "the one who is now called a prophet." And in 19:20 we see Samuel "standing in charge" of a company of prophets, although he does not seem to participate in their frenzied activity. Other than that, biblical usages of the word "prophet" for Samuel all come from later books.[1] But our identification of Samuel as a prophet does not rest on these explicit descriptions alone. We also think of him as a prophet because of the roles he plays in 1 Samuel, particularly his receipt and transmittal of communication from God.

Prophet is not, however, the only role Samuel plays. His actions, especially in 1 Samuel 7, also resemble those of a "judge," a charismatic war leader and governor. In the Hebrew text of 1 Samuel 12:11 (see the NRSV note) Samuel includes himself in a list of judge/deliverers. Hebrews 11:32 may intend the same thing when it mentions "Gideon, Barak, Samson, Jephthah, . . . David and Samuel and the prophets." Yet another identity, "priest" (someone who maintains the relationship between God and community, especially through rituals), is suggested by Samuel's relationship to Eli and offering of sacrifices.

There is probably no single right answer to the question of Samuel's role. Different sections of his story celebrate different roles for him. Furthermore the terms "prophet," "priest," and "judge" are ideologically loaded. The term "prophet," in particular, has had different implications for different people at different times. So in discussing whether Samuel was a "prophet," we need to ask, by which definition?

This chapter begins by examining the relatively clear terms "priest" and "judge," then moves on to "prophet," discussing each term's range of meanings and how well each term fits Samuel. Given the fluidity of the roles and the differing pictures our sources provide of Samuel, we cannot neatly sort his activities into clear definitional boxes. However, discussing these issues improves our understanding of Samuel's functions and the stakes of the storytellers who tell us about him.

PRIEST

Priests, in the world of ancient Israel, were specialists responsible for seeing that the community stayed in a positive relationship to the divine realm. Scholars often describe them as having three primary duties: performance of religious rituals (especially sacrifice), divination, and teaching (Blenkinsopp 1995, 80–83; Miller 2000, 165–71; notice that these are the three functions mentioned by the blessing on Levi in Deuteronomy 33:8–11). Priests are also described as being responsible for blessing the people and resolving disputes between people (Num 6:22–27; Dt 21:5 and 17:8–12). This section deals first with general biblical information on priests, then with the picture in 1 Samuel, and finally with how Samuel himself fits into the picture.

Our impression of biblical priests is a composite one based on writings assembled over the better part of a thousand years. During that period there were struggles over the priesthood. We see evidence of such a struggle in the oracles against Eli's house in 1 Samuel 2 and 3. Deuteronomy equates "priests" and "Levites" (the passages just cited speak of "the levitical priests" and "the priests, the sons of Levi"), while Ezra/Nehemiah and Chronicles speak of priests and Levites as separate groups. Ezekiel 48:11 contrasts "the consecrated priests, the descendants of Zadok, who kept my charge, who did not go astray" with Levites who did go astray. The Aaronite/Zadokite priests emerge from this struggle with firm control of sacrificial privileges, while judicial and teaching functions belong to the Levites (Num 18:1–3; 2 C 19:8–10 and 35:3).[2]

We should not assume that the presentation of priests in 1 Samuel conforms to the standards of much later periods. Judges and Samuel preserve stories from a period when the restriction of priesthood to Aaronite or even Levitical families is not yet firmly in place. The Ephraimite Micah appoints his own son as priest in Judges 17:5, and David does likewise in 2 Samuel 8:18. Most of the persons explicitly described as priests in the books of Samuel come from Eli's lineage: Eli himself, his sons Hophni and Phinehas, Ahimelech and the other priests of Nob, Ahijah,[3] and Abiathar. Even the priest Zadok, who serves alongside Abiathar in David's administration, is described as a descendant of Eli in 2 Samuel 18:17, although this verse's genealogical information seems scrambled.[4] Zadok may well have come from a totally different lineage, as do David's sons and probably Ira the Jairite (2 S 20:26). So although Samuel is an Ephraimite, not a Levite (1 S 1:1),[5] that in itself may not have barred him, at this time, from being a priest.

In the books of Samuel, priests do play the expected ritual roles. Eli and his sons preside over sacrificial festivities in 1 Samuel 1–2. Ahimelech in 1 Samuel 19 tends a shrine, judging from his mention of "bread of the Presence" in 19:6. Zadok and Abiathar are said to carry the ark (a cultic activity later reserved for Levites) in 2 Samuel 15:29. These activities link the priests with particular sacred places: Eli and his sons serve at the temple at Shiloh, Ahimelech's generation moves its base to Nob, and Abiathar and Zadok end up with the ark in Jerusalem.

Eli's pronouncements to Hannah in 1 Samuel 1:17 ("go in peace; the God of Israel grant the petition you have made to him") and Elkanah in 2:20 ("may the LORD repay you with children by this woman") probably qualify as blessings. Ahijah in 1 Samuel 14:18–19 and 36–42, Ahimelech in 22:15,[6] and Abiathar in 23:6–12 and 30:7–8 are asked to perform divination (asking LORD what is likely to happen or what action should be taken) for the leaders they serve. Several of these passages mention the Urim and Thummim (sacred lots) or ephod (the breastplate in which the lots were carried).[7] This is consistent with a general pattern of priestly divination being conducted by "technical" means using special equipment (Miller 2000, 185).

Later, in the accounts of Absalom's rebellion and Solomon's accession (2 S 15–19 and 1 K 1–2), the priests Abiathar and Zadok appear (along with the generals Joab and Benaiah and the prophet Nathan) as important supporters of various contenders for kingship. These stories show the political power that priests could wield.

What we do not see in the books of Samuel is any mention of priests, outside of Samuel himself, as teachers or as judges. I suspect that the emphasis on teaching and judging functions for priests comes primarily from Deuteronomic and Deuteronomistic thought, and the core Samuel narratives are older than that.

Nowhere in the Bible is Samuel himself explicitly called a priest. Psalm 99:6 comes closest, stating that "Moses and Aaron were among his [LORD's] priests" and then adding, "Samuel also was among those who called on his name."[8] Yet many think of him as a priest, partly because the story of his call (1 S 3) follows a statement that LORD will raise up "a faithful priest" (2:35), and partly because Samuel does perform some priestly functions.

The "faithful priest" passage is actually a false lead, so let us deal with it first. In 1 Samuel 2:35, LORD announces to Eli, via an anonymous "man of God," that Eli's house (lineage) will be cast off and "I [God] will raise up for myself a faithful priest, who shall do according to what is in my heart and in my mind" (2:35). This is immediately followed by the story of LORD's nighttime announcement to Samuel repudiating Eli and his descendants. We then hear that, "as Samuel grew up, the LORD was with him, and let none of his words fall to the ground. . . . The LORD continued to appear at Shiloh, for the LORD revealed himself to Samuel at Shiloh by the word of the LORD" (3:19 and 21).

It is understandable that many readers identify Samuel as the promised "faithful priest." But let us follow the playing out of the prophecy. The predicted disaster for

Eli's house arrives first in the death of his two sons in 1 Samuel 4, then in Saul's slaughter of the rest of the family in 1 Samuel 22. (Saul is angry because Eli's great-grandson Ahimelech has assisted David.) The one survivor of that slaughter is Ahimelech's son Abiathar, who takes refuge with David and his men (22:20) and provides divination services for David throughout David's wilderness period. Later in Jerusalem, Abiathar serves alongside another priest, Zadok. In 1 Kings 1:7–8, Zadok casts his lot with the winning aspirant to the crown, Solomon, while Abiathar supports David's eldest surviving son, Adonijah. Solomon retaliates by dismissing Abiathar from temple service and exiling him to the village of Anathoth outside of Jerusalem, "thus fulfilling the word of the LORD that he had spoken concerning the house of Eli in Shiloh" (1 K 2:27).[9] This narratorial comment clearly identifies Zadok, the claimed ancestor of Jerusalem's priests hundreds of years later, as the "faithful priest" anticipated in 1 Samuel 2:35.[10] Samuel, even if we were to decide he were a priest, is a far poorer match than Zadok for the description of the "faithful priest" for whom a "sure house" will be established. Neither he nor his sons are ever said to serve as priests for David (the definitive "anointed one") or even Saul, and the Deuteronomistic History mentions nothing of his subsequent descendants.[11]

Some have proposed that in ancient Israel, as in medieval Europe, "surplus" males would be dedicated to the priesthood, with Samuel a likely example of this (Stager 1985, 27–28). True, Samuel's mother gives him, as a young child, "to the LORD" (1:11 and 1:28). In concrete terms this means that she leaves him at Shiloh, a major worship and sacrificial center, "to minister to the LORD, in the presence of the priest Eli" (2:11). The Hebrew verb translated "minister" in this verse—it appears again in 1 Samuel 2:18 and 3:1— is often used to describe priestly service (for instance 1 K 8:11), although Numbers 8:26 (in which NRSV translates the verb as "assist") uses it for the work of Levites as distinguished from the unique "service" of priests. Samuel is also said, in 1 Samuel 2:18, to wear a "linen ephod," which verse 22:18 speaks of as if it were a garment typically worn by priest. David also wears a linen ephod (2 S 6:14 and 1 C 15:27), but one might ask whether David is performing priestly functions then.

Not everyone working at the Shiloh temple was a full-fledged priest. Notice the reference in 2:15 to the priest's "servant," *naʿar,* a word used repeatedly in 1 Samuel 1–3 for Samuel himself. To be sure, *naʿar,* which can mean either "boy" or "servant," is also used as a term for Eli's sons (2:17; "young men" in NRSV), but in 2:15 the *naʿar* is clearly distinguished from the priest. So Samuel's position at Shiloh is not necessarily a priestly one. After the Philistines destroy Shiloh—a destruction passed over in silence by 1 Samuel, but implied by Shiloh's disappearance from the story and the move of the priests—its priests move to Nob (1 S 22).

The fact that Samuel returns to his birth town, Ramah, and is never shown in association with Nob suggests that he was not one of the Shiloh priests.

On the other hand, after Samuel leaves Shiloh, we see him making offerings and blessing sacrifices (7:9–10, 9:13, 16:2–5, and perhaps 15:32–33), and he builds an altar in his home town (7:17). With respect to sacrifice, readers particularly notice 1 Samuel 13, where one possible interpretation of Saul's offense is that he offers a sacrifice himself rather than waiting for Samuel. However, sacrifice does not seem to have been limited to priests in this period. Biblical writers repeatedly speak of "the people" or particular individuals offering sacrifices: Hannah and Elkanah, David, and Solomon are all said to make sacrifices (1 S 1:26, 2 S 6:13, and 1 K 8:62–64). Although 1 Samuel 9:11–13 mentions townspeople who will not eat of their sacrifice until a holy man blesses it, the holy man is not called a priest, but a seer, which the narrator tells us is an earlier term for prophet (9:9). Some generations later Elisha's slaughtering of his cattle in 1 Kings 19:21 sounds a great deal like a sacrifice: recall that sacrificial meat is boiled in 1 Samuel 2:13–14 and notice the similarity to 1 Samuel 6:14 with regard to cooking sacrificed cattle on the wood of the implement they have been pulling. Even more unmistakably, 1 Kings 18:30–38 depicts Elijah making a sacrifice. These examples show that prophets, as well as priests, were at times considered suitable officiants at sacrifice (at least during some periods and by some groups). Thus Samuel's sacrifices cannot be taken as firm proof that he is a priest.

I have mentioned that priestly divination is ordinarily associated with the ephod and lots. While the "linen ephod" worn by Samuel in 1 Samuel 2:18 may have priestly overtones, it is never (in contrast to "the ephod") mentioned in connection with divination. The only passage that might associate Samuel with a priestly method of technical divination is 1 Samuel 10:19–24, where lots are cast to select a king. However, the language in this scene is strikingly passive: we hear who "was taken" by lot, but we do not know who cast the lots. I think that in this instance Samuel employs lots (likely cast by someone else) to distance himself from the choice. Normally Samuel is associated not with lots but with vision and word, the most common media for *prophetic* perception of Lord's messages: "the Lord continued to appear at Shiloh, for the Lord revealed himself to Samuel at Shiloh by the word of the Lord" (3:21).

Samuel does claim for himself the role of teacher (12:23; "I will instruct you in the good and the right way") and is described in 10:29 as writing the "rights and duties of the kingship" up in a book to be laid "before the Lord." In his teaching and writing he resembles Moses, but since Moses is a prophet from the priestly tribe of Levi, it is hard to say whether this parallel is priestly or prophetic. Since Samuel's other priestly activities (sacrifice, judging, and blessing) are ones that can also be performed by prophets, I would suggest that we see Samuel not as a priest in any narrow technical sense, but as a superprophet whose functions, like Moses's, extend into the priestly sphere.

JUDGE

In English a "judge" presides in a legal court or does other evaluative decision making. But the Hebrew verb *špṭ*, from which *šōpēṭ* ("judge") comes, can designate military and executive as well as judicial activity.[12] The Israelites use the verb in this broader sense when they ask Samuel to "appoint for us . . . a king to govern [*špṭ*] us" (1 S 8:5).

The usage of *špṭ*-family words in 1 Samuel has its context in the book of Judges. Some of that book's "judges," such as Deborah, may indeed "judge" in the usual English sense (Jdg 4:4–5). But most are depicted in terms of military might. Ehud's only reported activities are an assassination and leading the Israelites to kill ten thousand Moabites (3:12–30), and Samson seems more concerned with personal revenge than care for his people (Jdg 14–16). While NRSV and some other translations render *špṭ* as "judged" in the book's summary statements about various persons (for example, "Jephthah judged [*špṭ*] Israel six years"; 12:7), some other modern versions use "led" (NIV: "Jephthah led [*špṭ*] Israel six years"). I think "led" is a more accurate translation, although it may leave readers wondering why we call this the book of Judges.

The judges seem to have been tribal heroes (although for some, such as Samson, the term "hero" may be a stretch) whose stories typically involve one or just a few named tribes. The prose version of Deborah's story in Judges 3, for instance, mentions only the tribes of Zebulun and Naphtali, plus a woman from the allied but non-Israelite clan of the Kenites.[13] In some stories Israelite tribes fight each other, as in Gilead's war with Ephraim (Jdg 12:1–6) and the attacks on Benjamin in Judges 20. But the stories have now been packaged in a framework that lines the local heroes up as successive leaders of "all Israel." The book's guiding program appears in Judges 2:18–19: "Whenever the Lord raised up judges for them, the Lord was with the judge, and he delivered them from the hand of their enemies all the days of the judge; for the Lord would be moved to pity by their groaning because of those who persecuted and oppressed them. But whenever the judge died, they would relapse and behave worse than their ancestors, following other gods, worshiping them and bowing down to them. They would not drop any of their practices or their stubborn ways."

Subsequent stories follow this pattern. Judges 3:12 tells us that "the Israelites again did what was evil in the sight of the Lord" and are consequently oppressed by Moab. "But when the Israelites cried out to the Lord, the Lord raised up for them a deliverer, Ehud son of Gera" (3:15). Following the narrative of Ehud's exploits, we hear that "Moab was subdued that day under the hand of Israel. And the land had rest eighty years" (3:30).

Then "the Israelites again did what was evil in the sight of the Lord, after Ehud died" (Jdg 4:1). They were "sold" to a Canaanite king with iron chariots, and again they "cried out to the Lord for help" (4:3). Deliverance came through Deborah, with the assistance of a general named Barak and a Kenite woman named Jael, after which "the land had rest forty years," but then again "the Israelites did what was evil in the sight of the Lord" (Jdg 5:31 and 6:1).

Let me say a bit more about Judges because the book influences our understanding of Israel's need for a king, which is an issue central to Samuel's career. As Judges proceeds, the stories tell less and less of deliverance and more and more of highly problematic behavior: Abimelech's fratricide and ill-fated kingship in Judges 9; Jephthah's human sacrifice and promotion of intertribal violence in chapters 11 and 12; Samson's poor judgment with women and violent retaliations in 14–16; the making and stealing of an idol and its priest and the destruction of a peaceful city in 17–18; and gang rape, more intertribal warfare, and mass kidnapping of women in 19–21. The book ends with the statement that "in those days there was no king in Israel; all the people did what was right in their own eyes" (21:25).

All this can be interpreted in two ways, both relevant to 1 Samuel. One interpretation, often offered with a quotation of Lord's words to Samuel in 1 Samuel 8:7 ("they have rejected me from being king over them") or the reference in 1 Samuel 12:19 to "demanding a king for ourselves" as "evil," sees judges as God's preferred mode of government for Israel. In this view the book of Judges teaches that the people do not need a king. If they will be faithful, things will go fine; and even if they are not faithful, God will raise up deliverers when the people cry out. (This view has even been used to explain the intertribal warfare and kidnappings in Judges 20–21: "the people can solve their problems without a king.") This interpretation fits nicely with Noth's idea of a Deuteronomistic History that justifies God's destruction of the kingdoms, and it prepares us for the antikingship strand in 1 Samuel.

The other interpretation, which sits nicely with Cross's theory of a Josianic first edition of the Deuteronomistic History, often appeals to statements about David as Lord's chosen leader (see 1 S 13:14, 16:12–13, 25:28; 2 S 7). This interpretation sees Judges as a demonstration that the Israelites will not remain faithful without a king. In this view the closing statement in Judges about "no king in Israel" implicitly continues, "and we can see what a mess that was; they needed a king!" With this interpretation, we enter the books of Samuel already knowing that Israel needs a king.

While most readers choose one interpretation and ignore the other, we should remember the assertion of the literary critics that kingship is a complex question.

A story that only presented the case for or against would not be interesting or credible. A story that can be interpreted either way honors the complexity of the question.

Meanwhile, returning to the question of roles, the idea of the divinely raised judge (*šōpēṭ*) unifies the Deuteronomistic History's presentation of the transitional period between the people's establishment in the land and their emergence as a nation with a king.[14] Not only the leaders in Judges but several figures in 1 Samuel are presented in judgelike ways.

Although we think of Eli primarily as priest, his death notice in 1 Samuel 4:18 follows the format for judges: "He had judged [*špṭ*, NIV 'led'] Israel forty years." The use of classic judgeship language at the end of Eli's rule and the beginning of Samuel's suggests that the "Baals and Astartes" put away by the people in 7:4 were not worshipped during Eli's lifetime but were taken up in response to the ark's departure or the slaughter that accompanied its return, since in the paradigm of Judges, the people remain faithful during a judge's lifetime and fall away only in the interim periods. In addition to casting a positive light on Eli's leadership (though not his sons' behavior), the use of judgeship language for Eli in 4:18 reminds us that a character can fill more than one role.

Saul, too, fits the judge model well. Although the noun *šōpēṭ* is never used to describe him, he is appointed in response to the people's request for "a king to govern [*špṭ*] us" (1 S 8:5; the verb is used again in 8:6 and 8:20). Like Gideon (Jdg 6), Saul does not seek leadership but is summoned to it from his life as a farmer's son (1 S 9 and 11:5; he also has to be summoned in 1 Samuel 10:22). In 9:16 Lord says that Saul "shall save my people from the hand of the Philistines; for I have seen the suffering of my people, because their outcry has come to me." The scenario of Lord responding to the people's cry, as well as the specific term "save" (Hebrew *yšʿ*, often translated as "deliver"), hark back to the pattern in Judges, where *yšʿ* is used about as frequently as *špṭ* for the activity of deliverer judges. It is worth noticing the connection between Lord's announcement of deliverance through Saul and the people's hope in 7:8 that Lord will save [*yšʿ*] them from the hand of the Philistines. While 7:13–17 reports a reprieve from enemy incursions during the days of Samuel (prior to Saul), the statement in 7:13 that "the Philistines were subdued and did not again enter the territory of Israel" is clearly not the whole truth. In 1 Samuel 9, Lord still thinks that Israel needs a deliverer.

The depiction of Saul as judge/deliverer continues in the story of his victory over the brutal Ammonite oppressor Nahash (1 S 11; the introductory paragraph that appears at the end of 1 Samuel 10 in NRSV is not present in the Hebrew text and has been drawn from Greek manuscripts). Following a familiar pattern, the story begins with a report of oppression and resulting distress. When Saul (once again engaged in farm work) hears of the oppression, "the spirit of God came upon Saul in power." He hacks up his oxen (imagine a modern farmer smashing his best tractor) and sends the pieces "throughout all the territory of Israel" along with a summons to battle (11:5–8).[15] Saul then leads his recruits to victory against the Ammonites, prompting a joyous affirmation of his leadership at the end of the chapter. This depiction is capped by a summary of Saul's successful career as a deliverer who "did valiantly . . . and rescued Israel out of the hands of those who plundered them" (14:47–48). Only the opening phrase of this summary, "when Saul had taken the kingship," alerts us to the fact that he was a king rather than another in the sequence of judges.

There is plenty of other material, of course, that casts Saul's leadership in a less positive light. But the parts of his story that portray him in judgelike terms are deeply significant for us in two ways. First, they show Saul's career as a continuation of established Israelite traditions, rather than as a new and wicked initiative (contrast the attitude in Samuel's speech in 1 S 12). Second, and very important for our understanding of Samuel himself, the fact that both Samuel and Saul are described with terminology reminiscent of judgeship means that, as David Gunn has shown in *The Fate of King Saul,* when we think about Samuel's attitude toward the anointing of Saul, we need to think about human jealousy as well as theology (1980, 59).

To understand that point, however, we need to notice that Samuel, too, is described as a judge. *Špṭ* terminology is explicitly used to describe his activities in 7:6, "Samuel judged [*špṭ*, NIV 'led'] the people of Israel at Mizpah," and 7:15, "Samuel judged Israel all the days of his life," a statement much like the death notices in the book of Judges. Parallels between Samuel's birth story and Samson's also suggest that Samuel may be a judge. He uses *špṭ* to describe his own activity in 12:7, "therefore take your stand, so that I may enter into judgment with you" (although here the overtones may be more narrowly judicial). He even, in the Hebrew text, lists himself among successful judges: "Lord sent Jerubbaal and Bedan, and Jephthah, and *Samuel,* and rescued you out of the hand of your enemies on every side" (12:11, following NRSV notes, italics added; the Greek text has "Jerubbaal and Barak, and Jephthah, and *Samson*").

Chapter 7 is particularly striking in its characterization of Samuel as a judge. In the book of Judges, the people fall away from Lord and begin worshipping foreign deities, then return and are delivered from foreign military oppression by the judge. In 1 Samuel 7:3, Samuel calls Israel to "put away the foreign gods and the Astartes from among you," and they comply. The Philistines begin an attack, Samuel calls on Lord, "Lord thundered with a mighty voice" (7:10), and the Philistines are routed. According to the program of Judges, foreign oppression should now cease for the duration of Samuel's career, and 7:13–14 reports that "the Philistines were subdued and did not again enter the territory of Israel; the hand of the LORD was against the Philistines all the days of Samuel." Not surprisingly it is in the final verses of this chapter that we find the earlier mentioned statement, "Samuel judged Israel all the days of his life."

While 1 Samuel 7 clearly presents Samuel as a judge and a successful one, there is tension between this chapter and those surrounding it. Samuel's call for repentance comes as a surprise: nowhere else in 1 Samuel do we hear of defection from LORD to other gods. Furthermore, the assertions of 7:13–14 notwithstanding, the Israelites do not seem to enjoy peace for the duration of Samuel's life, The chapters between 7 and the notice of Samuel's death in 25:1 are full of strife among the Israelites, Philistines, and other foreign enemies. It also appears that Samuel did not "judge Israel all the days of his life," for although in 8:1–3 he appoints his sons as judges and, shortly thereafter, participates in Saul's installation as king, his death is not mentioned until 1 Samuel 25.

Almost every sermon I have ever heard on 1 Samuel 8—the chapter in which the people say to Samuel, "you are old and your sons do not follow in your ways; appoint for us, then, a king to govern [*špṭ*] us" (8:5)—has said that Samuel's resulting distress—"the thing displeased Samuel" (8:6)—was because the prophet believed the people were rejecting LORD, who was their proper king. But the issue of rejecting LORD is brought into the conversation by LORD, not Samuel: "they have not rejected you, but they have rejected me" (8:7). The fact that LORD begins by assuring Samuel that it is not the prophet they have rejected suggests that rejection of Samuel, not rejection of LORD, is what Samuel has prayed to LORD about (Gunn 1980, 59). When we realize that Samuel himself has been the one to *špṭ* Israel (7:15, 16, and 17) until growing old and appointing his two sons (8:1), we see something we may not have seen before: the people are asking Samuel to appoint someone different to the position he and his sons have held. This may also explain the pique we hear in Samuel's questions at the beginning of what will become his great antikingship sermon: "I have listened to you in all that you have said to me, and have set a king over you. See, it is the king who leads you now; I am old and gray, but my sons are with you. I have led you from my youth until this day. Here I am; testify against me before the LORD and before his anointed. Whose ox have I taken? Or whose donkey have I taken? Or whom have I defrauded? Whom have I oppressed? Or from whose hand have I taken a bribe to blind my eyes with it? Testify against me and I will restore it to you" (1 S 12:1–3).

The pique comes through again a few verses later, where, as we saw earlier, the Hebrew text (unlike the Greek text followed by NRSV) of 12:11 lists Samuel as one of four judges who have delivered Israel: "the LORD sent Jerubbaal and Bedan, and Jephthah, and *Samuel,* and rescued you out of the hand of your enemies on every side; and you lived in safety. But when you saw that King Nahash of the Ammonites came against you, you said to me, 'No, but a king shall reign over us'"

(11–12 following NRSV notes, italics added). When I myself was sent by LORD to rescue you, Samuel asks, how dare you ask instead for a king?

IDEAS AND IDEALS OF PROPHECY

In common English usage, a prophet is someone who predicts the future, with, in religious contexts, the further nuance that the prophet claims to have received the information directly from God. A second common usage portrays prophets as proclaimers of God's judgment against the status quo. Both of these views connect to biblical depictions of prophets as people "whose *primary function was to receive messages from the deity*" (Blenkinsopp 1995, 177, Blenkinsopp's italics). Beyond that, however, prophets have been and continue to be thought of in a variety of ways, many of which are highly idealized. Sorting through the diverse material on prophecy is easier if we can identify some of these idealizations at the outset.

One prominent line of modern idealization sees the prophet as a courageous advocate of justice who challenges the corrupt institutions, superstitions, and self-interested religion of the status quo. Typical passages quoted in support of this viewpoint are the following:

> I hate, I despise your festivals,
> and I take no delight in your solemn assemblies.
> . . . .
> But let justice roll down like waters,
> and righteousness like an ever-flowing stream. (Amos 5:21 and 24)

> "Will the LORD be pleased with thousands of rams,
> with ten thousands of rivers of oil?
> Shall I give my firstborn for my transgression,
> the fruit of my body for the sin of my soul?"
> He has told you, O mortal, what is good;
> and what does the LORD require of you
> but to do justice, and to love kindness,
> and to walk humbly with your God? (Mic 6:7–8)

People arguing the superiority of prophetic religion sometimes appeal also to these words of Samuel:

> Has the LORD as great delight in burnt offerings and sacrifices,
> as in obeying the voice of the LORD?
> Surely, to obey is better than sacrifice,
> and to heed than the fat of rams. (1 S 15:22)

It is usually assumed, when such material is quoted, that "burnt offerings" and "the fat of rams" represent priestly religion, a misguided enterprise in which God takes no pleasure, while justice, righteousness, kindness, and obedience are the virtues of the prophetic tradition.[16]

Such a view of prophecy was held by many American civil rights activists in the 1960s. They quite fiercely identified themselves with the prophets calling for reform, in contrast to their parents' churches, which they saw as blind to justice and as perpetuators of the status quo. Their tendency to see prophets as godly and priests as corrupt was supported by Protestant biblical scholars who identified themselves with the prophets and the Roman Catholic church with the priests. Indeed many biblical studies books, especially from the nineteenth and early twentieth centuries, say things about the superiority of prophetic over priestly religion that have little to do with ancient Israel and a lot to do with Protestant stereotypes of Catholicism. This scholarly polemic built in turn upon a long-standing Christian tradition (visible already in the gospels) of identifying Christianity with the prophets and "ritualistic," "legalistic" Judaism with priests. Never mind that many Jews identify as strongly with "ethical monotheism" as liberal Christians do. This gives us the following set of ideological identifications:

	Prophets	are to	priests
as	reformers	are to	corrupt institutions
as	Protestants	are to	Roman Catholics
as	Christians	are to	Jews
which is as	good	is to	bad.

I certainly do not endorse these valuations, but I do think it important to recognize them because they continue to influence, often without our being aware of it, contemporary understandings of prophets and priests.

A variant of the social justice understanding emerges in the emphasis in the recent literature on the "marginal" position of prophets, especially in the cases of prophets who practice group and ecstatic prophecy (Blenkinsopp 1995, 130–34; on the cross-cultural background, see Lewis 1978 and 1986). More "classical" prophets such as Amos, Micah, and Isaiah, the great figures of the eighth century B.C.E., have also been characterized as speakers "on behalf of the socially and economically disadvantaged," although these prophets themselves may very well have come from more privileged classes (Blenkinsopp 1995, 147; see also Wilson 1980 on "central" and "peripheral" prophecy). Micah was likely a member of a landowning class with considerable political power (Blenkinsopp 1995, 158). Isaiah moves freely among Jerusalem's highest officials and may have been a priest himself, judging from the setting of his inaugural vision in Isaiah 6. The term "shepherd" or "sheep breeder" used for Amos (1:1) describes the king of Moab in its only other biblical appearance (2 K 3:4), suggesting that Amos was not simply a poor peasant farmer. Later, as we have seen, "prophetic" voices seem to unite with the king and the priests of Jerusalem in support of Josiah's reform (Blenkinsopp 1995, 155–63), which quite breaks down any idea of systematic opposition between prophets and royal interests. The role of a woman, Huldah, in the reform shows that even in this period a person who would not normally have had access to high councils could have influence as a prophet, but we cannot simply assume that everyone called a prophet is engaged in activity on behalf of the marginalized.

Both modern and ancient Christian and Jewish idealizations of prophets build upon idealized notions of prophecy in the Bible itself. At a fairly late point in the compositional history, the term "prophet" comes to be used to describe almost any religiously good person. So, for instance, Genesis 20:7 calls Abraham a prophet—in the context of intercessory prayer, which will also be a theme in the stories about Samuel—and the verb "prophesy" is used for the singing of Levitical musicians in the temple (see 1 Chronicles 25:1–3, although note that there is also a connection between prophets and music in 1 Samuel 10:5 and 2 Kings 3:15). A New Testament speech attributed to Peter refers to David as a prophet (Acts 2:30).

The Deuteronomistic History is not quite so wide in its usage, but it does clearly identify Moses as a prophet, whose like can be expected to reappear in a later time (Dt 18:15–18 and 34:10). Against biblical traditions that associate *tôrā* (which literally means "teaching") with priests and "word" with prophets (for example, Mic 3:11 and Jer 18:18), in the Moses traditions Torah *is* prophetic word. That the Deuteronomistic historians do not assume conflict between prophets and establishment officials such as priests and king can be seen with particular clarity in 2 Kings 22:14–20, where king and priests turn to the woman prophet Huldah for verification of the "book of the Law" that the priests have just brought to King Josiah. I suspect that the positive relationships between prophet, priests, and king in this story reflect a positive relationship between the compilers of the Josianic layer of the Deuteronomistic History, who I think regarded themselves as prophets, and the Jerusalem priests and king who stood to benefit from the Deuteronomistic program of centralizing worship and emphasizing Lord's covenant with David.

In the Prophetic Record on which the Deuteronomistic History was likely built, however, we find more tension between prophets and establishment authorities.[17] While prophetic support of particular kings is implied by the Prophetic Record's stories of prophetic anointings and while the prophets are clearly close enough to the centers of power that they have access to kings, the stories also depict prophets proclaiming divine rejection of kings (even kings, such as Saul, whom the prophets themselves anointed). They do not justify their actions by appeal to ethical principles or the authority of Torah. Instead the prophets are depicted—by the narrator and in the reported speech of the prophets themselves[18]—as delivering messages received directly from Lord. The authenticity of their access to the divine realm is shown in this layer by, among other things, their ability to issue correct predictions of the future (a criterion also mentioned in Deuteronomy 18:22). Thus this layer of the story supports the idea of prophecy as prediction empowered by direct personal contact with Lord.

Conflict with authority is a frequent (although not universal) theme in the books that the Jewish canon calls the "Latter Prophets": Isaiah, Jeremiah, Ezekiel, and the twelve short books from Hosea to Malachi. (Daniel, included among the prophets in Christian sequencings, appears in the Writings section of the Jewish canon.) But here we run into something odd. None of these "prophets" actually refers to himself as such, and only five are called prophets in introductory verses or narratives about them (Blenkinsopp 1995, 128). A number of them rage *against* prophets. Micah says the message of prophets depends entirely on who feeds them (Mic 3:5). Amos, whose line about letting "justice roll down like waters" (Amos 5:24) makes him the paradigmatic prophet for many, denies that he is a prophet (*nābî'*):

> [The priest] Amaziah said to Amos, "O seer, go, flee away to the land of Judah, earn your bread there, and prophesy there; but never again prophesy at Bethel, for it is the king's sanctuary, and it is a temple of the kingdom." Then Amos answered Amaziah, "I am no prophet, nor a prophet's son; but I am a herdsman, and a dresser of sycamore trees, and the Lord took me from following the flock, and the Lord said to me, 'Go, prophesy to my people Israel.'" (Amos 7:12–15)

Amaziah is angry because Amos has said that "the high places of Isaac shall be made desolate, and the sanctuaries of Israel shall be laid waste" (7:9). Thus Amos fits both of today's common ideas about prophets: he has made a prediction, and he is in conflict with an established religious authority. Amaziah calls Amos a "seer" (*ḥōzeh*, not the same Hebrew word as in 1 Samuel 9:9, but very similar in meaning), although alongside it he uses a verb closely related to the noun "prophet." It is Amos who introduces the term "prophet" (*nābî'*), and apparently not in a complimentary sense: "I am no prophet, nor a prophet's son." Yet Amos describes his God-commanded activity with the same verb that Amaziah used in his rebuke (*nb'*; 7:12 and 15).

Why does this exemplar of prophecy deny being a prophet? One way to solve the conundrum is to have him say something different, and so NIV (in keeping with its habit of smoothing things over in translation) reads "I *was* neither prophet, nor a prophet's son" (12:14, italics added). This is technically possible, since the Hebrew text has no explicit verb at all (it says, "not prophet I and not prophet's son I"). However, when the verb "to be" is missing—as it usually is in

Hebrew—we normally supply it in the present tense, as do the NRSV, RSV, NJB, TNK, and NLT editors.[19]

The NLT, in a paraphrase that prioritizes reader understanding over word-for-word principles of translation, interpretively expands Amos's words. In its paraphrase, Amos says, "I'm not one of your professional prophets. I certainly never trained to be one." This rendering understands "son of a prophet" to mean "belonging to a group of professional prophets." ("Group of prophets" is how NLT translates a related phrase in 1 Kings 20:35 and 2 Kings 2–9; NRSV and NIV, by the same logic, give us companies of prophets in those chapters). The NLT translators believe—in my view correctly—that Amos is not making a statement about his family connections, but about his professional identity.

To get an idea of what Amos may be denying, look at 1 Kings 22. The kings of Judah and Israel sit enthroned while four hundred prophets (22:6; compare "the four hundred fifty prophets of Baal and the four hundred prophets of Asherah" in 1 Kings 18:19) predict success in an upcoming battle. At least one prophet wears iron horns to show how the kings will gore their opponents (22:11). But the king of Judah, who would really rather not participate in this battle, asks that one more prophet be summoned. The summoning messenger warns this prophet, Micaiah ben Imlah, to say what the king wants to hear. Micaiah initially does so. When exhorted to tell the truth, however, he describes a scene in which Lord asks who will "entice" the Israelite king into a fatal battle (22:20). A spirit proposes (according to Micaiah), "I will go out and be a lying spirit in the mouth of all his prophets" (22:22). Lord endorses the plan, and "so you see," Micaiah tells the Israelite king, "The Lord has put a lying spirit in the mouth of all these your prophets; the Lord has decreed disaster for you" (22:23). The king responds by ordering that Micaiah be imprisoned. Here we see group prophecy, symbolic action, flattery of the king, and a dissident individual who declares disaster for the king, all in a single story.

How is one to know a "true" prophet from a "false" one?[20] Although modern individualism quickly seizes on the image of Micaiah standing alone against the group, the theme of individual versus group is not a consistent indicator of prophetic validity (or, at least, validity in the eyes of the writers who give us the Bible). Some "true" prophets are members of groups. Samuel himself may be linked to the group that experiences "prophetic frenzy" in 1 Samuel 10:10–11, and he is explicitly "standing in charge" of such a group in 1 Samuel 19:20–24, although the description of Saul's activity under the group's influence is hardly complimentary. Elisha, too, is described as leader of a company of prophets (2 K 6:1). So when we see prophets operating in groups we cannot automatically conclude that they are "false." Nor can we assume that if prophets are priests or work in an "establishment" setting such as the temple, they must be false. David's prophets Nathan (1 K 1) and Gad (1 S 22:25 and 2 S 24:11) seem to have been regular members of his staff. Isaiah clearly has access to the highest centers of power (Isa 7); Jeremiah prophesies in the temple itself (Jer 28); and Ezekiel is a member of the temple priesthood. Colorful activity such as dressing in horns is also not a mark of false prophecy: such greats as Isaiah, Jeremiah, and Ezekiel also engage in symbolic behaviors (see for instance Isa 8:1–4, 20:1–2; Jer 27:2, 28:10; and Ezek 4–5).

Nor can a message favorable to established authorities be automatically disqualified as false. Although Jeremiah 28:8–9 suggests that a true prophet is more likely to utter words of doom than hope (a pattern generally born out in the canon), we do see some positive prophecies from true prophets, such as Nathan (2 S 7) and Isaiah (Isa 7:1–16; 2 K 20:4–11). Indeed the entire middle section of the book of Isaiah (Isa 40–55) is a glowingly optimistic prophecy. Most historical-critical scholars attribute those chapters to an exilic writer (usually called Deutero-Isaiah or Second Isaiah) rather than to the prophet Isaiah in the eighth century B.C.E., but even if they do come from a different source, these chapters testify to the belief (on the part of some, anyway) that true prophecy could contain good news.

Even the criterion of whether a prophet's predictions come true (Dt 18:21–22; Jer 28:9) does not quite succeed in distinguishing those prophets who the canonical writers consider false from those who seem to be considered true. Isaiah's initial prediction of Hezekiah's imminent death, delivered in "thus says the LORD" messenger format, does not come true (2 K 20:1–11). Neither, according to 2 Kings 24:6, do Jeremiah's predictions that Jehoiakim will go unburied and have no heir (Jer 22:19, 36:30). Ezekiel 26:7–21 clearly states that Tyre will fall to Nebuchadrezzar, but Ezekiel 29:18–20 tells us that Nebuchadrezzar will get Egypt instead, since his campaign against Tyre failed. (Alexander the Great finally conquered the city centuries later.) In the Micaiah ben Imlah story (1 K 22), the "lying" message delivered by four hundred prophets is itself commissioned and approved by LORD. But the criterion of fulfillment has one additional, and significant, problem: even to the extent that it is reliable—and it is not completely so—it is useless to the people who must decide which prophet to believe before the events have transpired.

The discussion so far makes clear, I hope, that the Bible supports a variety of common ideas about prophecy. The most consistent theme across the various depictions is the idea of a prophet as announcer of an inspired message.[21] The messages are sometimes unsolicited announcements about the choosing or deposing of leaders or warnings and calls for repentance. But sometimes, as in the Micaiah story (1 K 22) or David's consultation of Gad in 1 Samuel 22:25, leaders specifically ask prophets for oracles on tactical questions. Saul asks for such counsel and does not get it (1 S 28:6 and 15). In this regard prophets and priests share a function, although the two use different divination methods.

Beyond this, prophets may be members of groups or stand (so far as we know) unaccompanied. They may be associated with particular cultic places or simply arrive as the man of God does in 1 Samuel 2:27. Their behavior may but does not have to be quite colorful. They may or may not deliver news favorable to established authorities. Prophetic predictions of the future often come true, but not always. Some prophets are associated with miraculous happenings (for example, the resurrection occasioned by contact with Elisha's bones in 2 Kings 13:20–21 and the shadow moving backward in 2 Kings 20:11); others are not. We hear several stories of healings (for instance, Elijah's resurrection of a widow's son in 1 Kings 17:17–24 and Elisha's healing of Naaman in 2 Kings 5:1–19). Intercession is also mentioned as a prophetic activity, as for instance in the comment in Genesis 20:7 that because Abraham is a prophet he can be expected to pray for Abimelech, and as in the challenge in Jeremiah 27:18 that "if indeed they are prophets . . . then let them intercede with the Lord of hosts." Because of the variety of ways in which prophets are presented, we need to pay close attention to see which descriptions fit Samuel and which do not, in which stories.

SAMUEL AS PROPHET

Samuel unquestionably fits the most general definition of a prophet as a person to whom Lord speaks and who conveys Lord's word to others. But which of the array of more specific functions ascribed to prophets does he perform?

Blenkinsopp comments, "Of all the roles assigned to Samuel, the one that appears to be historically the least suspect is that of 'father,' that is, abbot or sheik of a mantic group whose ecstatic behavior seems to have been contagious (1 Sam 19:18–24)" (1995, 133). In the incident Blenkinsopp references, David has fled from Saul to Samuel at Naioth. Saul sends messengers after him and finally goes to Naioth himself, but upon encountering a group of prophets there, the messengers and Saul himself fall into "prophetic frenzy." Samuel himself is "standing in charge" of the group. Connection between Samuel and an ecstatic group may also be implied by 10:5–6, where Samuel predicts that the newly anointed Saul will meet "a band of prophets coming down from the shrine with harp, tambourine, flute, and lyre playing in front of them." Here too, when Saul meets the band, the spirit of God comes "mightily" upon him and he joins their "prophetic frenzy" (10:10–12), prompting onlookers to ask, "is Saul, too, among the prophets?" However, Samuel's leadership of the band is not clearly asserted.

To be in or fall into "prophetic frenzy" is NRSV's way, in these passages, of translating a Hebrew verb, *nb'*, that corresponds to the noun "prophet," *nābî'*, The same Hebrew verb is used to describe Saul's behavior in 18:10, where an "evil spirit from

God" overtakes him and he throws his spear at David, although in that story NRSV translates *nb'* as "he raved" (KJV translates it, "he prophesied"). "Raved" probably gives an accurate picture of the behavior, but it fails to convey the verb's association with the noun "prophet." In the books of Samuel, persons in such "prophetic frenzy" do not deliver predictions or social critiques; it is not clear whether they even speak. In 19:20–24 one could argue that the frenzied prophesying performs a God-intended function in that it saves David from arrest, but it is hard to argue that Saul's frenzy-incited spear throw in 18:10 is helpful to anyone. While Samuel's association with frenzied prophecy may be a historically accurate note, it is a minor motif in the final story, and the storytellers never depict Samuel himself in frenzy.

A much stronger influence on our perception of Samuel as prophet is the call story of 1 Samuel 3, which explicitly introduces the term "prophet" (3:20). The chapter emphasizes Samuel's receipt of the "word of the Lord" that had been "rare" under Eli and that Samuel himself had not previously encountered (3:1, 7). The chapter also tells us that "*visions*" had not been widespread in Eli's day, but that after Samuel's establishment as a prophet, "the Lord continued to *appear* at Shiloh" (3:1 and 21, italics added). Similar mixing of word and vision language appears often in connection with prophets (note the reference in Isaiah 2:1 to "the word that Isaiah . . . saw"). The call story's closing statements that "the Lord was with him and let none of his words fall to the ground," "the Lord continued to appear," and "the word of Samuel came to all Israel" (3:19–4:1) imply that a lot of prophesying followed this initial incident. However, the only specific message that we hear Samuel receive or pass along concerns the rejection of Eli's house. So at this point, our impression of Samuel's prophetic role is weighted toward the prophet as someone who declares Lord's support of some leaders or withdrawal of support from others.

First Samuel 9 speaks of a "man of God," also referred to as a "seer" (*rōʾeh,* a word that suggests the seeing of visions). In the present version of the story, this seer is Samuel (also referred to as a seer in 1 Chronicles 9:22, 26:28, and 29:29), although in an earlier version, the seer may have been anonymous. Verse 9 tells us, believably, that seer is an older term for "prophet." This story and 1 Samuel 3 are the only passages in the books of Samuel that explicitly assign prophetic status to Samuel. (The prophetic-frenzy passages discussed earlier link Samuel to prophets and their activity but without actually stating that he participates in it.)

The statement in 1 Samuel 9:9 about prophets and seers is a bit puzzling, since at this point in the narrative the word "seer" has not yet been used (Saul and his servant initially talk about a "man of God"). The explanation may be that the Hebrew word "prophet" in 9:9, *nābīʾ*, is in form identical to the word "we bring," *nābīʾ*, used by Saul in 9:7. Locating the explanation close to Saul's statement might be an editor's sly stab at prophets who "see" for pay, or the resemblance between the words could have been simply the trigger that reminded the editor to insert an explanation. I am inclined to the second theory, as I think the editor wants to elevate rather than downgrade Samuel.

At the beginning of 1 Samuel 9, Saul's servant describes the seer as someone who might, for a fee, be able to locate lost donkeys. The villagers look to him to bless their sacrifices. These two functions probably belong to the original layer of the story. A third element, probably present originally as the seer's announcing of Saul's kingly destiny to him, has been strengthened in the present version so that Samuel not only tells Saul about kingship but formally anoints Saul king-designate. It is probably in connection with Samuel's role as kingmaker that the editorial voice in 9:9 is so eager to have us know that the "seer" is actually a prophet. Notice, then, that both stories that actually use the term "prophet" (1 S 3 and 9) concern the anointing or deposing of leaders. The role of anointer-and-deposer will also figure heavily in the famous stories of Samuel's confrontations with Saul (1 S 13 and 15) and his anointing of David (16:1–13), and these events will be referred to by Samuel's ghost in 1 Samuel 28, although the word "prophet" is not used for Samuel in these other chapters. In the stories of Samuel's power to appoint and depose leaders, a secondary theme emerges about his discomfort with the role and occasional disagreements with Lord.

Prediction of the future is a relatively minor role for Samuel, and his predictions always serve some other agenda. I would argue that this is true for all the prophets of the Hebrew Bible but will focus here on Samuel. The fulfillments of Samuel's short-term predictions in 10:1–9 and 12:16–18 (the conclusion to Saul's anointing and Samuel's "farewell speech") serve as signs authenticating his message: the prediction of the man of God about the deaths of Eli's sons, 2:34, also uses the language of "sign." In connection with signs, we should perhaps notice that Samuel—unlike Elijah or Elisha—never performs a healing or feeding miracle.

The prediction by Samuel's ghost that "tomorrow you [Saul] and your sons shall be with me; the Lord will also give the army of Israel into the hands of the Philistines" (28:19) simply rubs salt in Saul's wounds: it is hard to imagine that at this point he really expects anything else, and the information is useful to no one. In Samuel's pronouncements of divine election and rejection, statements such as "you shall reign" or "your kingdom will not continue" are less predictions than alternative ways of stating what has already happened: "the Lord has anointed you" or "the Lord has sought out a[nother] man after his own heart" (10:1, 13:14). In Samuel's exhortations to the people, statements such as "direct your heart to the Lord . . . and he will deliver you," "you will cry out . . . but the Lord will not answer you," or "if you still do wickedly, you shall be swept away" (7:3, 8:18, 12:25) are intended to motivate rather than present otherwise unknowable data. In fact, in these cases the future seems not to be fixed, but dependent upon the people's response. Prediction is not Samuel's central business.

Social justice is an even less prominent theme than prediction. While we often see Samuel exhorting the people or Saul to obey LORD, the only speech in which he speaks of how Israelites are treated by their leaders (or how they treat one another) is his diatribe against kingship in 8:10–18, which characterizes a king as one who "will take" all kinds of things from the people. Samuel does not say that this taking would be offensive to LORD. Rather he seems to hope that the people's own aversion to such activity will prompt them to withdraw their request for a king. Theologically the problem Samuel names with kingship is that it is a rejection of LORD as king (10:19, 12:12; compare LORD's similar comments on the subject in 8:7–8).

The theme of respecting and obeying God is strong in Samuel's speeches. Samuel never condemns Saul for taking from the people—nor have we any reason to believe that Saul did so, Samuel's dire warnings notwithstanding. Instead Samuel complains that Saul disrespects LORD's (or Samuel's) commands (13:13–14, 15:17–26). Samuel's warnings and exhortations to the people also seem more focused on LORD's honor than on LORD's ethical expectations, as he calls upon them to turn away from other gods (7:3) and obey LORD (12:13–16 and 20–25) without reference to what LORD wants them to do. If LORD had a track record in the books of Samuel or even the Deuteronomistic History of commanding social justice, we might be justified in reading such an interest into Samuel's talk about obedience. As we shall see, however, these narratives do not show LORD as someone with a particular interest in the poor or oppressed.

At the same time that Samuel emphasizes LORD's demands for obedience from the people, he presents himself, and is spoken of by the people, as one who can intercede with LORD on their behalf (7:8–9, 12:19–23). This is a role mentioned elsewhere for prophets, and several verses outside of 1 Samuel mention Samuel's power of intercession (Ps 99:6, Jer 15:1, Sir 46:16–17, and 2 Esdras 7:108[22]). The exploration of LORD's character in the next chapter underlines why intercession is such an important issue.

SUMMARY

Although the stories in 1 Samuel use the word "prophet" for Samuel just twice, they certainly present him as someone to whom LORD speaks and who tells the people about LORD's wishes and decisions. In this regard "prophet" is the single best designation for Samuel's role. He conveys LORD's decisions about other leaders (Eli, Saul, and David), in keeping with the Prophetic Record's ideal of the prophet as anointer and denouncer. However, Samuel is also a leader in his own right, a judge (especially in 1 S 7) and perhaps priest (especially in 1 S 2–3) who governs the people, guides their military affairs, and claims authority to teach them. In this combination of roles he resembles Moses and Joshua and reinforces the conception of the Josianic layer of the Deuteronomistic History that there is no necessary conflict between the roles of governor, priest, and prophet. In the exilic layer of the Deuteronomistic History, Samuel's ability to combine roles may illustrate the hope that in the absence of kings, powerful religious leaders can guide the nation and keep it safe.

In this powerful presentation of Samuel, the recollection of him as leader of an ecstatic band of prophets has dropped almost out of sight. Although Samuel does oppose kingship, we do not see from him the advocacy of social justice that so many people admire in the books of prophets such as Amos and Micah. Nor is Samuel primarily a predictor of the future, although in the service of other purposes he does do some predicting. Unlike Moses, Elijah, or Elisha, he never performs healings or feedings. He does function as an intercessor, and occasionally he gets into disagreements with LORD. I will return to these two themes later.

CHAPTER 4

THE PROBLEMATIC GOD OF SAMUEL

The survey of Samuel and his roles has revealed a consistent emphasis on Samuel's standing as a spokesperson for LORD. He receives revelation by vision and word, ending an era in which such revelation has been rare (1 S 3). He announces the withdrawal of divine support from particular families and individuals (Eli and his house in 1 Samuel 3, Saul and his house in 1 Samuel 13, 15, and 28) and enacts the commissioning of those whom LORD has chosen to be new leaders of the people (Saul in 1 Samuel 9–11, David in 1 Samuel 16). But Samuel is not only portrayed as an adviser to leaders. He himself leads the people (1 S 7–8 and 12). And at points the narrators, the people, and Samuel himself make little distinction between Samuel's leadership and LORD's.

This close connection between the leadership of Samuel (whether via direct rule or his say in who else will rule) and of LORD means that our perceptions of Samuel tend to be colored by our feelings about LORD's rule. Although most Bible readers assume that their feelings about LORD's rule should be positive, many nonetheless feel uneasy, and for good reason. This chapter focuses on how LORD is portrayed in the books of Samuel, centering the discussion on the story of Samuel (1 S 1–16, 19:18–24, 25:1, and 1 S 28),[1] with discussion of texts elsewhere in the books of Samuel or the Deuteronomistic History when I believe that the original authors or their editors had such texts in mind. I also cite parallels at points where a reader might say, "Surely a biblical writer would not depict God that way!" In such cases, supporting examples help establish that the themes I point out really do recur. In general my conclusions here match those of my article on the depiction of LORD in 1 and 2 Samuel (Steussy 2000), except that here, where I barely touch upon the texts that deal with David, the theme of God's favor for David naturally looms less large.

WHAT LORD DOES

Both Judaism and Christianity, as we know them, speak of God as loving. Today God is also generally depicted as concerned with the personal lives of individuals. In the Samuel stories, LORD does speak to, punish, or support individuals (notably Eli, his sons, Samuel, Saul, Jonathan, and David), but with the single exception of Hannah, all the individuals involved are priests, prophets, judges, and kings. Furthermore, and again with Hannah's case as a possible exception, LORD acts more as a warlord than as a loving father toward these leaders and the people.

We can see this most clearly, perhaps, by simply listing what the Samuel narrator says LORD does. I focus on what the narrator says not because I understand biblical narrators to be infallible—I do not believe that they are—but because if we are trying to understand how LORD is portrayed *in the narrative,* the narrator's (or narrators') statements are the "gold standard" for our answer. What characters say is important, too, and often characters seem to act as mouthpieces for the narrator. This seems likely, for instance, in Hannah's speech (1 S 2:1–10). But we also have to reckon with the possibility that a character might be, relative to the narrator's baseline, lying or misinformed, either because a narrator intends this effect or has been careless or because the work of different narrators has been merged.[2] We should not simply assume that a character's words represent the narrator's viewpoint.

Here is a list of actions attributed directly to LORD by the narrator in the stretch of narrative under review. In cases where the narrator notes LORD's speaking or not speaking presented as a datum in itself, I include it on this list. Speeches in which LORD is actually quoted are discussed later.

1:5–6	LORD closes Hannah's womb.
1:19–20	LORD remembers Hannah; she conceives.
2:21	LORD takes note of Hannah; she has five more children.
2:25	LORD prevents Eli's sons from listening to their father.
3:1	LORD does not speak ("word of the LORD was rare").
3:4–14	LORD calls to Samuel, reveals condemnation of Eli.
3:19,21	LORD is with Samuel, lets none of Samuel's words fall to the ground, reveals self to Samuel.
5:6	LORD's hand heavy on Ashdod; terror and tumors result.
5:11–12	LORD's hand heavy on Ekron; panic and tumors result.
6:19	LORD kills 70 (or 50,070) Beth-shemeshites.
7:9–10	LORD answers Samuel; thunders against, confuses, and routs Philistines.
7:13	LORD's hand is against Philistines all the days of Samuel.
10:9–10	LORD gives Saul "another heart," spirit upon him, throws him into prophetic frenzy.
10:26	LORD touches warriors' hearts so they follow Saul.
11:6–7	LORD's spirit is on Saul, "dread" on Israelites so they follow Saul.
12:18	LORD sends a thunderstorm on day of the wheat harvest.
14:15	"Panic of God" falls on the Philistine garrison.
14:23	LORD gives Israel victory.
14:37	LORD does not answer Saul.
16:13–14	LORD withdraws spirit from Saul and places it on David, sends evil spirit to torment Saul (also 16:23, 18:10–14, 19:9).

19:20–24	LORD sends spirit to put Saul and his messengers into prophetic frenzy.
28:6	LORD does not answer Saul by dream, lot, or prophet.

Events implicitly attributed to LORD but without explicit confirmation include the following:

4:2 and 10	Philistines defeat Israel.
1 S 5–6	Dagon statue falls and breaks; panic and tumors arise among the Philistines.
6:12	Cows pull cart with ark straight to Israelite territory.
1 S 9	Saul is guided to Samuel.
10:9	Signs announced by Samuel are fulfilled.
10:20–22	Saul is chosen by lot.
11:11	Ammonites are defeated.
14:41–42	Jonathan is identified by lot.
14:47–48, 15:7–8	Saul achieves more victories (as does David in subsequent chapters).

Notice the types of action attributed to LORD. Except for the giving of children to Hannah and, perhaps, the guiding of cows to Israelite territory (although what happens when they arrive is not pretty), LORD's means of action tend to be destructive even when the results are favorable to Israel—which is not always the case. When LORD sends spirit upon leaders, violent action usually follows (military victories or, in the case of the evil spirit sent upon Saul, attacks on David). While LORD's military interventions sometimes work to Israel's benefit, at other times LORD supports Israel's enemies. Being the recipient of LORD's attention is not necessarily beneficial for an individual: LORD closes Hannah's womb, destroys Eli's family, elevates Saul to a kingship that will destroy him, and identifies Jonathan by lot after Saul vows to kill whomever the lot falls upon (although in this case the army saves Jonathan). One might say that this LORD knows more about making war than making peace, or, as an ancient bit of biblical poetry more concisely puts it, "LORD is a warrior" (Ex 15:3).

A focus on national issues (the various military interventions) and on leaders is obvious in this list. The apparent exception is LORD's involvement with Samuel's mother, Hannah. Because it comes at the very beginning of Samuel's story, this incident helps set our expectations for what is to come.

LORD AND HANNAH: CARING FOR THE LITTLE PEOPLE?

Does not Samuel's opening story of a wife's unhappiness over her childlessness and later celebration at the birth of a son show that LORD does care for and intervene on behalf of ordinary individuals? My answer to that question is "yes, and no." The chapter invites us to focus on Hannah from the second verse, which names her (when a wife is named, we know a story will follow) and tells us that she has no children. The details about Peninnah's tormenting, Elkanah's love, and Hannah's own distress—so memorably articulated in her prayer/vow—enhance the story's human interest. We wince when Eli censures Hannah for drunkenness and cheer when she corrects, however obsequiously, his misperception. We are delighted to hear of the birth of her child (1:20), although the story does not end with the birth but continues until Hannah fulfills her vow to give her son back to Lord (1:28). This story does elicit concern for Hannah, and Lord's response to her allows the conclusion that Lord is interested in not only the great and mighty, but also the needy whom Lord lifts "from the ash heap" (2:8).

Yet each time I read the report of the fulfilling of Hannah's vow, "they slaughtered the bull, and they brought the child to Eli" (1:25), I shudder at the parallel between the slaughter of the bull and the handing over of the child. Samuel and the bull are both three years old, probably,[3] and both are now lost to Hannah and Elkanah. If Hannah wants to raise a child, rather than just bear one, the story is not over until 2:19–21, where we learn that she has other children and maintains at least some continuing relationship to this one.[4]

If we look beyond the bare fact of the granting of the child to Hannah, the depiction of Lord in this story might give us pause. Hannah seems to think of Lord as someone whose favor can be won by gifts: "if you will give to your maidservant . . . then I will give him to Lord" (1:11, my translation; the words rendered "give" and "set" by NRSV are actually the same verb). "What sort of god does Hannah have faith in?" ask Danna Fewell and David Gunn. "A god who only gives when he gets something in return? A god who requires a mother to give up her child in order to live up to society's conditions of value?" (1993, 138). Furthermore, while Lord does reverse Hannah's barrenness (1:19–20), Lord was, according to verses 5 and 6, responsible for that barrenness to begin with. Polzin (1989, 21) questions this evaluation, suggesting that "Lord had closed her womb" in these verses is not the narrator's opinion but "concealed reported speech" from Elkanah (1:5) and Peninnah (1:6). His explanation is possible, especially in 1:6 where we can easily imagine Peninnah's taunt, "Lord closed your womb!" However, the narrator gives us no reason to doubt the characters' ascription of responsibility to Lord, and Hannah's own song (2:1–10) will underscore Lord's responsibility for ill fortune as well as good.

At this point allow me to note that I think the ancient writers attribute the womb closing to Lord because they assume that all events can be attributed to Lord or spirits authorized by Lord (such as the "evil spirit" afflicting Saul and the "lying spirit" in the Micaiah ben Imlah story). Today many people understand infertility as a medical problem produced by natural laws operating in a morally blind fashion, something that just happens rather than something imposed by a specific decision of God. Our concept of "natural law," however, is a relatively modern one. People of the ancient Near East certainly noticed regularities in nature—the sun rising and setting and seasons running their course—but they seem to have imagined more direct divine involvement in these cycles than we do. (Notice LORD's promise, in Genesis 8:21–22, that the cycles will continue.) They certainly interpreted storms, droughts, illness, and barrenness as the direct actions of the divine. And since such events often harm people who appear innocent, attributing such events to the gods led to the conclusion that the gods were, at least sometimes, unpredictable and unfair.

Even today, of course, some hold spiritual forces responsible for infertility. Those who believe this generally assert either that God has caused the problem for some good, but perhaps undiscernable, reason or that the devil is at work, leaving us to wonder why God permits such mischief. Such ideas are so embedded in our thinking about God's action that we easily read them into everything we see. So, when modern readers hear a psalmist say, "[D]o not rebuke me in your anger" (Ps 6:1), they tend to assume that the psalm is a prayer for forgiveness (thus the presence of Psalm 6 in Western Christianity's list of "penitential psalms"). If LORD is angry, the psalmist must have sinned, the modern logic goes, and so in praying for healing and an end to anger (6:3), the psalmist must be repenting. But Psalm 6 contains no confession of sin. It is likely a prayer for physical healing, and I believe that the illness itself is what leads the psalmist to think LORD is angry. There is no evidence that the psalmist knows what has triggered this anger, much less that he or she considers it deserved. The psalmist is not repenting; he or she just wants the pain to end (Steussy 2004, 78–79). Psalm 44, a communal lament, also attributes disaster to LORD without assuming that the ill treatment is deserved. "You have rejected us and abased us, and have not gone out with our armies," say the psalmists to LORD, ". . . yet we have not forgotten you, or been false to your covenant" (Ps 44:9 and 17). To Christians in particular (since Christianity has taught that everyone is sinful and deserves punishment) it may seem outrageous to accuse LORD of rejecting without cause, but the psalm does so. We need to keep this in mind as we read 1 Samuel. For ancient people, saying that LORD did something bad to a person did not necessarily imply that the person deserved the bad fortune, nor did it necessarily imply that LORD had some good purpose in mind.

Let us go back to Hannah's story. Caught up in the emotional motifs of family conflict and motherhood, a modern reader may easily fail to notice how highly stylized the story is. It probably has less to do with the feelings of a historical Hannah, if there was one, than with the culture's ideas of how a barren woman *ought* to feel and react. Furthermore, in the ancient world, the motif of a hitherto-barren woman giving birth seems to have been a standard opening for the story of a man with a special destiny, a national ancestor or savior.[5] Hannah's story echoes that of Rachel and Leah (rivalry between a beloved barren wife and her fertile co-wife) and, even more, that of Samson's mother, via the motifs of no razor touching the child's head and the mother not indulging in wine or strong drink.

Not shaving the head and not drinking alcohol are features of the so-called nazirite vow ("nazirite" is a Hebrew word meaning "dedicated" or "consecrated") described in Numbers 6:1–21. The Hebrew text of Samuel transmitted in Jewish tradition does not use the term "nazirite" in 1 Samuel 1, but the word does appear in a Qumran Samuel scroll and may also have appeared in the Hebrew text from which the ancient Greek translation was made.[6] On this basis NRSV uses "nazirite" in its translations of both Hannah's vow and her dedication speech (1:11 and 22).

As described in Numbers, however, the vow covers a limited period of time and is made by the person who is going to do it. Only in the cases of Samson, Samuel, and possibly the Rechabites of Jeremiah 35 (see also 2 K 10) do we find people committed to such a vow prior to birth or having to abide by it for life. The prohibition against haircutting will figure prominently in Samson's later life, but a nazirite-like status is never mentioned again for Samuel, strengthening the suspicion that the motif appears in Hannah's speeches as a pointer linking this birth story to Samson's and thereby alerting us that Hannah's child will be a judge/deliverer.[7]

In Samson's story the angel who announces the upcoming birth sets the nazirite conditions, while in Samuel's story Hannah sets them. David Jobling asks whether Hannah herself may not have had the tradition of the barren woman's son as leader in mind. He suggests that she commits her son to Lord and nazirite practices precisely because she wants "a son being prepared for a position of leadership in Israel" (1998, 132; Jobling also points out [133], that we do not even know whether she or her husband want the additional children she bears in 2:21). But regardless of whether we see Hannah as "an ambitious woman who . . . hopes to satisfy her ambition vicariously through her son" (Jobling 1998, 132), the barren-woman theme does create expectations about the son's destiny.

One other very odd pointer toward leadership issues occurs in 1 Samuel 1. Hannah repeatedly uses the verb "to ask" (*š'l*). For instance, in 1:20 she explains Samuel's name by saying, "from Lord I have asked him" (my translation), although this does not actually fit the name Samuel, which means, "his name is El" or "his name is God." In 1:28, when Hannah presents Samuel to Eli, NRSV renders her words as, "I have lent him to the Lord; as long as he lives, he is given to the Lord," but the words translated as "lent" and "given" are actually, again, forms of the Hebrew verb "ask." One might translate it: "I have made him be asked-for by LORD; as long as he lives, he is asked-for by LORD." The exact Hebrew form of the verb's second occurrence in this verse, "asked-for," is *šāʾûl*—which just happens to be, in Hebrew, Saul's name. In other words the emphasis on "asking" (some of which is hidden in translation by terms such as "given" and "lent") relates much more directly to Saul's name than Samuel's. The historical-critical scholar P. Kyle McCarter Jr. thus concludes, "Samuel's birth narrative has absorbed elements from another account describing Saul's birth" (1980a, 62–63). Others contest McCarter's conclusion, but whether or not pieces of Saul's birth story have crept into Samuel's, ancient audiences surely noticed the presence of Saul's name. The pun would have underscored the coming association between Hannah's child and the king.

Robert Polzin, a literary critic interpreting in the context of the completed Deuteronomistic History, reads Hannah's story as a political parable: "Hannah's request for a son is intended to introduce, foreshadow, and ideologically comment upon the story of Israel's request for a king" (1989, 25). For Polzin, Elkanah's tone of "loving understanding mixed in with feelings of hurt" in 1:8 symbolically represents LORD's feelings about Israel's request for a king (23). I am less sure than Polzin that ancient audiences would have made this connection. I do think that they would have picked up on the mention of Eli's sons in 1:3 and remembered from previous hearings of the story that these sons were corrupt and about to be cast off, creating a leadership vacuum. This detail, plus the traditional associations of barren-women stories with the births of nationally important figures and the more specific allusions to Samson's birth (via nazirite motifs) and Saul (via "asked" puns) would have sent, I think, a fairly strong signal to the audience that this story was not primarily about Hannah but about Israel's leadership (or lack thereof).

LIFTING THE POOR: HANNAH'S SONG (1 SAMUEL 2:1–10)

Hannah's song in 2:1–10 is described by many interpreters as "programmatic" for the books of Samuel. Historical critics generally agree that the song was not part of the original narrative, partly on the basis of the textual disruption in the verses just before and after it, but largely because "the lyrics presuppose the monarchy" (McCarter 1980a, 57–58 and 75). Although by metaphorical stretch we can apply the language of enemies and victory to Hannah's conflict with Peninnah, the song's opening line, "my strength is exalted . . . I rejoice in my victory" (2:1, with some textual uncertainties about the last word) would sit better in the mouth of a king than that of a woman giving away her firstborn child. The song's closest tie to Hannah's own situation lies in 2:5, "the barren has borne seven," but Hannah herself has so far borne only one child, and even at the end of the story she will have only six (2:21). Since the question of kingship for Israel has barely been broached (and then ambivalently, in the book of Judges) and Samuel himself will make some of the Bible's firmest statements against it, it is strange that his mother finishes her poem with the lines, "He [Lord] will give strength to his king, / and exalt the power of his anointed" (2:10). Carol Grizzard says in the *New Interpreter's Study Bible,* "This poem is a national thanksgiving and does not specifically relate to Hannah's situation. . . . It probably dates from a later period . . . than the book of Samuel" (2003, 396). Even David Toshio Tsumura, whose recent commentary on 1 Samuel consistently defends the unity and early date of most of the text, prefaces his judgment that "the Song fits well into the story of Hannah" with a concessive "whatever its original life situation may be" (2007, 136).[8]

According to Walter Brueggemann, the song in its present form declares "that Yahweh will reorder social reality, precisely in the interest of those too poor and too weak to make their own way" (1990, 20). He says it invites us to "watch while the despised ones (Israel, David) become the great ones. At the center of this startling inversion is the eighth son (16:11–12), who sits with princes and inherits a seat of honor (2:8)" (1990, 21). David, however, is no "despised one." He is, according to 1 Samuel 16:18, known as "skillful in playing, a man of valor, a warrior, prudent in speech, and a man of good presence" even prior to his arrival in Saul's court, and his father is rich enough to send bribes to his sons' commander (17:17–18). Even if David did start as one of the little people (which I doubt), he has moved beyond that position by the time Hannah's song is composed, let alone set into her story. So while the song overtly celebrates a God who helps the powerless, it covertly recruits our support for an already-powerful leader.

Jobling, more wary than Brueggemann about the present version of the song, bluntly ascribes it to "the royal propaganda machine," which is "very adept at creating the fiction that the king is on the side of the poor" (1998, 168). Yet Jobling argues that there is a "contradiction between the closing words in 2:10 and the general tendency of the rest of the song. The central section (vv. 4–8) celebrates Yhwh's liberation of the oppressed in terms compatible with a theology of revolution. Identifying herself with the oppressed, Hannah sings of how Yhwh acts to reverse sociopolitical dichotomies, taking power from those who have it and giving it to the (militarily) weak, the hungry, the barren, the poor. Celebration of these reversals forms the substance of the poem" (1998, 167). Like Brueggemann, Jobling hears in the song a fundamental commitment on Lord's part toward the least, the last, and the lost.

If Jobling is right, then the middle verses of the song add a social justice element to the Samuel books' characterization of Lord. I think, however, that we need to ask a couple of questions about this analysis. First, to what extent do even the middle verses really support a theology of liberation for the oppressed? Second, does the narrative that follows Hannah's song support its characterization of Lord as one who raises the poor from the dust?

With respect to the first question, some of the beneficiaries of Lord's actions in the middle verses—the feeble, hungry, barren, poor, and needy—are indeed socio-economically oppressed. But other lines, such as "Lord kills and brings to life" (2:6), involve no particular socioeconomic preferences on Lord's part. I think the entire section may be more about Lord's power to change things than about Lord's ethical or social commitments. Of course, for those who have nothing to lose, the hope of change, to say nothing of the hope of dramatic social reversal, may be attractive indeed. Meanwhile we should notice that the talk in 2:7 of making poor and making rich, bringing low and exalting, could easily support an argument that if there are poor and rich, Lord must have made them so; thus the social order we have must be the one Lord wants. Such a reading would fit the royal application, where any lifting of the poor to sit with princes (2:8) has already happened, at least for the poem's audience.

The second question is whether Lord does, in the books of Samuel, raise up the needy. The short answer is, no. When Lord does help underdogs, Lord is typically, as in the case of Hannah's barrenness, responsible for the problems they face. This pattern occurs frequently in the books of Samuel (Steussy 2000). The falling of Lord's spirit upon Saul in Samuel's presence protects David (1 S 19:23; see also 23:14), but it is Lord who provokes Saul's persecution of David to begin with.[9] In 2 Samuel 17:14, Lord saves David from Absalom's rebellion by defeating Ahithophel's good counsel, but the rebellion itself is Lord's punishment of David as announced in 2 Samuel 12:10–11. In 2 Samuel 21 and 2 Samuel 24, Lord delivers Israel from famine and plague, but in both chapters it is also Lord who initially imposes the troubles. Lord may raise the poor from the dust, but in the books of Samuel, at least, Lord puts them there to begin with.

The poor, in the books of Samuel, are most often casualties of Lord's interactions with the elite, although readers usually do not notice because they are caught up in the stories of the leaders. Focused on the playing out of predictions about Eli's corrupt sons, how many in the audience even notice that 34,000 Israelite soldiers also die (1 S 4:2 and 10; Eslinger 1985, 175)? Eager to absolve Lord, we might speculate that Israel has been complicit in the sons' sins. But according to 1 Samuel 2, the sons were remiss in their duties to the people as well as to Lord (2:13–14), and it is "the people" who tell Eli about the problem (2:22–24; Eslinger 1985, 125). In the events of 1 Samuel 4 and many that follow, the people must pay for the misdeeds of the leaders Lord has chosen for them. The people do presumably benefit from military victories achieved under Samuel, Saul,

Jonathan, and David. Yet at the end of 1 Samuel, the Philistines hold the field. By the end of 2 Samuel, the nation has suffered multiple internal rebellions, presaging its split into two nations after Solomon's death. By the end of the Deuteronomic History, both Israelite nations have fallen.

Randall Bailey likewise concludes that Lord does little in the books of Samuel to lift up the needy. Lord works by installing leaders, and the performance of those leaders (including Samuel) is problematic. "The prophets are either afraid or misrepresent Yhwh. The kings are either ineffectual or abuse power," Bailey says. "The reader is left to ponder who this Yhwh is who keeps choosing leaders with such clay feet" (1995, 227). He suggests that Jews in exile (whom he understands to have been the target audience of the Samuel books) likely regarded their own leaders as having performed no better. He then proposes that for the exilic audience, the point of Hannah's song (and its partner poem in 2 Samuel 22) was this: "If your (exilic) leaders are like this, do not give up hope. God can still reverse" the situation (1995, 227). I have heard a similar sentiment from students who admit having problems with how Lord is portrayed in 1 and 2 Samuel and elsewhere, but go on to say, "I want a God who is powerful, even if arbitrary and unfair, because what other hope is there for overturning the world's unfairness?"[10]

Hannah's song cannot imagine Lord as anything but a prince, a thundering Lord who shatters opponents but grants protection and favors to supporters. I believe this is because its composers have not experienced and cannot imagine social power structured otherwise.[11] Reversal of oppression, rather than its elimination, is the best outcome they can envision. At one level this is understandable: for those presently on the ash heap, the idea of being elevated to sit with princes is of course appealing. But in the world described by 2:4–8 (let alone 2:1–10), oppression remains. There are still princes and rich people on the one hand and hungry day laborers, forlorn mothers, and poor people on the other. The imagination of this song does not encompass a world where no one is hungry or lives on an ash heap and where no one "sits with princes" because there are no princes.

Understanding why reversal imagery and the depiction of God as a mighty king might be attractive leaves open the question of whether our imagination can or should be constrained by limits that pertained more than two millennia ago. Many cultures in today's world celebrate principles of participatory government. Granted, we are far from achieving oppression-free societies: abuse of social power by those of privileged gender, race, wealth, sexual orientation, education and other factors continues to be a problem. But if we have not achieved a world without poverty, war, hunger, and class exploitation, we can at least imagine and affirm the desirability of such a world. It strikes me as irresponsible to celebrate a simple reversal paradigm once we have asked whether we could we eliminate the structures of oppression entirely. Reversal language does not help us imagine how to accomplish that. How Hannah presents Lord in her song is one question. Whether our own understanding of God should conform to that presentation is another.

LORD'S ATTITUDES

Asking about Lord's attitudes, feelings, and motivations provides another angle on the characterization of Lord in the Samuel stories. We have noted Hannah's belief that Lord will give her a child if she promises to give the child back to Lord. The events of the story appear to confirm her belief. It is possible, of course, that Lord would have granted her a child even if she had not made the promise, but the close correspondence between the language of her vow ("remember me . . . then I will set him before you"; 1:11) and the language of the fulfillment ("Lord remembered her"; 1:19) suggests that her words have had an impact. Eli also seems to believe that Lord is likely to reward Hannah's giving back of the child, when he says to Elkanah, "may the Lord repay you . . . for the gift that she made" (2:20). We cannot be sure that Eli is a reliable commentator, since he was wrong about Hannah being drunk. But his assurance to Hannah about the fulfillment of her original request (1:17) and his blessing with regard to further children (2:20) are both followed by births, and in 3:8–9 his advice to Samuel is rock solid. Eli seems to know what he is talking about with respect to Lord.

The Offenses of Eli's Sons (1 Samuel 2–3)

The episodes concerning Lord's rejection of Eli's family tell us much about Lord's opinions. Eli's sons, we learn from the narrator in 2:12–13, are remiss in their actions toward both Lord and the people. But Lord's reported evaluation, "the sin of the young men was very great in the sight of the Lord; for they treated the offerings of the Lord with contempt" (2:17), involves only one part of their two-part offense.[12] Nothing is said about their mistreatment of the people, which reinforces the question raised in the discussion about Hannah's song of whether the Samuel stories actually depict Lord caring for people abused by their rulers. One might respond, of course, that the sons' sins against the people *are* sins against Lord. While this may be true elsewhere in the canon, there is so little support for this in the Samuel books that I think introducing it here is eisegesis, the reading in of our own theology rather than reading out of the text.[13]

Lord's displeasure with Eli's sons is next addressed by Eli himself. Eli believes that mediation is available for those who sin against people. In the Hebrew text, Eli even says Lord will mediate in such cases (2:25; see the NRSV note). But Eli questions whether there can be intercession on behalf of those who sin against Lord. Eli's distinction between sins against Lord and sins against humans suggests that the emphasis in 2:17 on the sons' offense against Lord (as opposed to their mistreatment of the people) is not accidental. Looking ahead for a moment, such a distinction might also explain why Lord reacts so strongly to Eli's sons' offenses while remaining silent with regard to the offenses of Samuel's sons (8:3): Samuel's sons offend only the people, not Lord.

The next report on Lord's feelings with regard to Eli's sons comes from a "man of God" (2:27–36). This is not a direct narratorial report. However, the man of God's speech employs a messenger format, and as far as I have been able to determine, prophetic reports delivered in formal messenger style ("thus says the Lord," "oracle of the Lord," and so forth) are never contradicted by the narrator of the Samuel books. The man of God's report agrees with our other information about Lord's opinion: Lord does not like being disrespected. "Why . . . honor your sons more than me? . . . Those who honor me I will honor, and those who despise me shall be treated with contempt" (2:29–30). Lord's sense of insult prompts the overriding of a promise that had been supposed to last "forever" (2:30). Lord will replace Eli's family with a "faithful priest," who will do what is in Lord's "heart and mind" (2:35).

Lord's speech to Samuel in 1 Samuel 3 again focuses not on abuse of the people but on sins against Lord: "because his sons were blaspheming God" (3:13; although as we saw, Lord's charge that Eli "did not restrain them" is problematic). Lord's denial of the possibility of expiation (3:14) confirms Eli's earlier suggestion that mediation is impossible for offenses against Lord (Fokkelman 1993, 178).[14] Lord's anger, at this point, appears implacable.

Defeat and Recovery (1 Samuel 4–7)

In 1 Samuel 4–6 we can only guess at Lord's motives and desires. Why does Israel suffer defeat at the hand of the Philistines in 4:2 and 10? No direct explanation is given, but the way in which the defeats interlace with fulfillment of the oracles against Eli's house suggests that the defeats are because of Lord's irritation with Eli's sons. One might object that Lord would not abandon thousands of soldiers to death just to punish a couple of errant leaders, but such scenarios occur over and over in the books of Samuel (and in the Deuteronomistic History more generally). Remember that at this point we are looking closely at what the books of Samuel say about Lord, not what we might believe about Lord from other sources, even biblical ones.

Since the book of Judges often describes defeats as Lord's response to being abandoned by the people (see Jdg 2:14, 3:8, 6:1, and 13:1), some readers look ahead to 7:3–4, where the people "put away the Baals and Astartes," and suppose that the Philistine victories in 1 Samuel 4 are Lord's punishment of Israel for worshipping other gods. However, 1 Samuel's use of judge language for both Eli and Samuel suggests that we should not imagine that foreign gods were worshipped during Eli's lifetime. Lyle Eslinger reaches the same conclusion on other grounds, noting that in Samuel's call for return to Lord (7:3) we hear nothing about previous defeats having been caused by faithlessness, "but only that putting the other gods away is a condition for future deliverance from the Philistines" (1985, 234; with a reference to Willis 1971, 303). Eslinger argues that "prior to Yahweh's action in 6.19 [smiting the Beth-shemeshites] the Israelites appear still faithful to Yahweh (e.g. 6.13–15). Following 6.19, however, they voice a Philistine-like objection to the presence of Yahweh and the ark (6.20); they put it (and him) in cold storage (6.21–7.1), and they mourn Yahweh's passing. With Yahweh dead and gone, Israel might well have turned to the reluctant worship of other deities" (1985, 234). Eslinger's phrase "Philistine-like" refers back to an earlier observation that in smiting the Beth-shemeshites, Lord treats Israelites just as Lord has treated the Philistines during the ark's sojourn in the Philistine cities (1985, 218). Eslinger says that although in Judges Lord does abandon the people because they have turned to other gods, here the people turn to other gods because Lord has abandoned Israel to defeat, to loss of the ark that symbolizes Lord's presence, and to sudden death when the ark returns (Eslinger 1985, 235). Lord eventually answers Samuel's cry on the people's behalf, but only afer they have repented and Samuel has offered a suckling lamb (7:4–10). Is this another instance of Lord's fondness for gifts?

Lord's response to Samuel's prayer in 7:9–10 marks a striking turn in the fortunes of Israel, which according to 7:13–14 enjoys peace for the rest of Samuel's life (although that assertion is, as we have seen, contradicted by later chapters). In light of Lord's warrior identity and conspicuous absence of concern for the people's internal affairs in 1 and 2 Samuel, it may be significant that while Lord subdues the Philistines, it is Samuel who "administers justice" (7:17).

Why Does Lord Give Israel a King? (1 Samuel 8)

In the story we are covering, the most perplexing passage with regard to Lord's desires is Lord's response to the people's request for a king. Lord says that "they have rejected me from being king over them" (8:8). So why, then, does Lord tell Samuel to "listen to their voice" (8:7, 9, and 22)?

The most common answer takes its cue from "they have rejected me" and Samuel's later reference to the people's request for a king as "wickedness" (12:17). In this interpretation Lord grants the people's request (or instructs Samuel to do so) in order to punish the people for their earlier rejection. Samuel's words about all the "taking" a king will do (8:11–18) will give Lord grounds to reply, when the people later complain about their king, "I told you so." The people's refusal to listen to Samuel's warning shows, in this reading, their stiff-neckedness. The phrase "like other nations" in the people's request for a king (8:5) shows that they are rebelling against the special covenant status, different than other nations, that Lord desires for them: "They are exchanging their true glory for status in the eyes of the world," says Tsumura (2007, 249).

The king-as-punishment interpretation makes fairly good sense of 8:7–22, although it conflicts with passages that describe kingship as Lord's plan for the people's deliverance. Such variation in the attitude toward kings is one of the main reasons for the historical-critical suspicion that 1 Samuel has been assembled from sources with significantly differing viewpoints. I think the source critics are almost certainly correct in positing multiple sources, but I am sympathetic with literary critics who argue that we must at least try to make sense of the final version.

These literary critics typically ask us to attend to the people's reasons for wanting a king. Things have not gone well, broadly speaking, in the book of Judges or in 1 Samuel so far. Following the leaders provided by Lord has taken the people to the point where they claim, "You [Samuel] are old and your sons do not follow in your ways" (8:4). There is a legitimate need for someone other than Samuel and his sons to *špṭ* (to judge, govern, or deliver).

Indeed, given how badly things have gone, perhaps there is legitimate need not simply for a new *šōpēṭ*, "judge," but for an entirely different system of leadership. Thus Eslinger, while agreeing with conventional wisdom that the request for a king "like other nations" is a rejection of Israel's special covenant status, says that the narrator has framed the story to let us know that the people's request is nonetheless justified: "The narrator himself . . . presents the misdeeds of Samuel's sons as legitimate cause for the Israelites' request" (Eslinger 1985, 263 and 261). Eslinger hears more than a hint of displeasure in Lord's response, but he does not assume that the narrator agrees with Lord. "The fact that Yahweh uses the verb *mā'as* [reject] to describe the rejection does not characterize the narrator's evaluation but Yahweh's" (1985, 263). Fokkelman similarly insists that we not confuse characters' evaluations with the narrator's. With regard to Lord's responses in 8:7–8, he suggests that "God's feeling rejected is a striking case of anthropopathy [attributing human feelings or suffering to God]. He suffers and feels himself abandoned, like a lover by the loved one. . . . Samuel is advised to brace himself and to be sure not to feel under personal attack. But these words of consolation and support come from a character who does not take his own advice" (1993, 340). Both of these interpreters see Lord, in this chapter, as willfully blind to the people's governmental problem. However much Lord may tell Samuel to listen to the people, Lord self is not doing so.

Robert Polzin offers a gentler interpretation of LORD's position and a harsher reading of the people's request. Speaking of "the mysterious forbearance of God and the continuing perfidy of God's people" (1989, 81), Polzin suggests that LORD (unlike Samuel, whom Polzin describes as "obstructive in a self-interested way") speaks in a tone foreshadowed by Elkanah's in 1 Samuel 1:8. "Oh Israel, am I not worth more to you than ten kings? Your desires here are so like your previous idolatrous deeds. Nevertheless, I will grant your request" (84, 87). According to Polzin, in this chapter "the narrator paints the picture of a God who reveals his love in spite of being rejected, in contrast to a judge who fails to conceal his selfish reluctance to become the maker of kings" (88).

Peter Miscall challenges the assumption that LORD feels rejected in this particular instance. Miscall observes that in Deuteronomy, the desire to have a king, even "like other nations," is anticipated without censure (1 S 8:5 and 20; Dt 17:14; Miscall 1986, 47). He says LORD's talk of being rejected in 1 Samuel 8:7–8 "does not refer specifically to the people's demand for a king but rather to their consistent abandonment of him to serve other gods. . . . The Lord is presenting Samuel with an analogy, not a particular accusation against the people. As the people have abandoned him to serve other gods, so they are abandoning Samuel to serve another leader; as the Lord still continues with the people, so should Samuel" (Miscall 1986, 48).

The probing of LORD's role in 1 Samuel 8 shows how much depends on which details (inside and outside the chapter) we take as our guides to interpretation. Eslinger and Fokkelman emphasize how problematic their special covenant status has been for the people, who suffer at the hands of divinely appointed leaders (such as Eli's sons) and then die by the thousands during LORD's punishment of those leaders. These interpreters see the people's desire for change as legitimate and well grounded. LORD's view of it as rejection then appears as divine touchiness. Polzin and Miscall see LORD trying hard to meet the needs of a consistently ungrateful people, but their interpretation requires that they see Samuel's objections primarily in terms of his own selfishness.

Jobling is sharply critical of this interpretive trend. It assumes, he says, that Samuel is wrong to oppose LORD's decision to give the people a king, while "the question of the *merits* of YHWH's will remains unasked" (1998, 64, Jobling's italics). In Jobling's judgment, kingship was "a disaster in its real historic effects," and he believes that, as the situation is presented in 1 Samuel 8, both LORD and Samuel know that it will be a disaster (65).

But why then does LORD tell Samuel to make them a king? Here Jobling focuses on the self-contradiction in LORD's response to the people's request: "YHWH first states that the people have rejected him *but not Samuel* (8:7), and then instantly retracts this by saying to Samuel, 'Just as they have done to me . . . *they are now doing to you*' (v. 8). This symptom of confusion has not been sufficiently attended to by commentators. It is a signal that YHWH is torn in two" (62, Jobling's italics). Jobling explains that in their desire to get rid of the judgeship system,

> the people have indirectly rejected YHWH. . . . But YHWH . . . wants to see the people's request as a *direct* uncomplicated rejection of himself. So he stumbles over his words. Worse, having gotten into this fix he stubbornly insists that the people must have their way even when they cease to want it [1 S 12:19]. YHWH passes from confusion to petulance and punitiveness. He is punishing the people for reminding him of words of his own [Dt 17:14–20] that he wanted to forget! (62, Jobling's italics)

With regard to the characterization of LORD, I think Jobling is right on two points. First, I appreciate his emphasis on the "confusion" in LORD's response (LORD first says that Samuel is not being rejected, then agrees that he is being rejected) and its effect on our impressions of the divine character: "from confusion to petulance and punitiveness." As Fokkelman says, LORD's urging that Samuel not feel rejected comes "from a character who does not take his own advice" (1993, 340).

Second, I appreciate Jobling's diagnosis of what is happening in the narrative. Rather than either simply attributing different views to different sources or attempting to explain the roughness in terms of a coherent artistic plan, Jobling attributes the text's incoherence to the insolubility of the problem the biblical writers are wrestling with. "Israel's history can be made coherent only on the assumption that YHWH gave permission for a form of government [kingship] of which he disapproved. But this does not make theological sense" (1998, 62). The Bible here wrestles with a question it cannot answer—one that it perhaps cannot even name. In its wrestling, it leaves LORD looking inconsistent and vindictive. In the end I follow the common reading: LORD is sure that kingship will not be good for the people, but LORD is huffy enough to impose it on them anyway. This is, however much I may not like it, consistent with other depictions of LORD in the Samuel books. LORD's touchiness about personal insult overrides whatever concern LORD may have about the welfare of the people.

Saul as LORD's Agent of Deliverance (1 Samuel 9–11)

In striking contrast to 1 Samuel 8, where LORD appears to experience the request for a king as a rejection, 1 Samuel 9–11 portrays LORD as initiator and supporter of kingship. Earlier we looked at 9:16, where LORD tells Samuel, "I will send to you a man. . . . He shall save my people from the hand of the Philistines, for I have seen the suffering of my people, because their outcry has come to me." In the next verse, LORD identifies Saul as the deliverer. Any sense of LORD grudgingly granting the king as a punishment is conspicuous by its absence.[15] Instead LORD responds to the people's outcry (same word as Exodus 3:7 and 9), although as usual LORD does so by means of a human leader.

In 10:1–8, Samuel affirms LORD as one who anoints rulers in order to save the people. He also lists a series of incidents that will happen to Saul, after which "the spirit of the LORD will possess you, and you will be in a prophetic frenzy . . . and be turned into a different person." After this, Saul is to "do whatever you see fit to do, for God is with you" (although Samuel then adds a possibly conflicting set of instructions for Saul to go to Gilgal and wait for Samuel to show him what to do). LORD follows through on Samuel's speech in 10:9–11 by giving Saul "another heart," after which "the spirit of God possessed him." This sequence, along with its follow-up in 1 Samuel 11, shows us a LORD who acts, in apparently good spirits, on behalf of the people's (not just their leaders') well-being, although as usual in the books of Samuel the problem and solution are both military in nature.

The Mizpah assembly in 10:17–26 has a darker tone. Because Samuel's speech in (10:17–19) is introduced with a messenger formula, "thus says the LORD," I think we are to take it as a narratively reliable quotation of LORD's words. However, since biblical Hebrew has no quotation marks, it is not clear where or whether LORD's words end and Samuel's begin. According to the translators who determined NRSV's punctuation, only the description of past deliverances comes from LORD, continuing the image of LORD as a deliverer (9:1–10:16) and allowing us to hold onto the notion that LORD is enthusiastic about Saul, as confirmed by Samuel's words in 10:24 and LORD's touching of warriors' hearts in 10:26. With this punctuation, it is Samuel, not LORD, who says that the people have rejected LORD (10:19).

The NLT interprets it differently, presenting the entire speech from "I brought you" to "tribes and clans" as a quotation of what LORD says. In its presentation, the statement about rejection (which does, after all, agree with what LORD said in 1 Samuel 8:7) comes from LORD, not just Samuel. This punctuation supports the interpretation that LORD really does not want a king at all.

The uncertainty about what to attribute to Samuel and what to attribute to LORD in 10:17–19 raises questions much like those we faced in 1 Samuel 8. How alike or different are Samuel's and LORD's responses to the request for a king? Does LORD bestow kingship as a positive solution to the people's problems, grant it as a reluctant concession, or intend it as punishment for what LORD perceives as rejection? An obvious option would be to interpret 10:17–19 in accord with the interpretation chosen in 1 Samuel 8. Since I have said that I think LORD sounds offended in 1 Samuel 8, using this strategy, I would attribute the statement about rejection (10:19) to LORD and not just to Samuel. Yet if I am reading 10:17–26 in the context of the rest of 1 Samuel 9–11, which seems very positive toward kingship, there is much to be said for NRSV's punctuation, which attributes the rejection comment to Samuel and leaves open the question of LORD's perception.

In the end I find myself wanting an interpretation that acknowledges historical-critical observations about the presence of different voices. To do so, I do not have to take a position on the exact dating of the different layers or read them in isolation from each other. Instead I simply imagine the Samuel story being told by a series of different tellers rather than a single performer. Someone (whom I might whimsically imagine wearing a "PROPHETS RULE!" T-shirt) has just told a story about how unhappy Samuel and LORD are about Israel's request for a king (1 S 8). Then someone else (possibly wearing a button that says, "Go Saul!") breaks in to tell us how LORD let Samuel know that Saul was the man to save Israel (9:1–10:16). In response, the first teller, or perhaps someone else on the same bench, tells about the Mizpah assembly (10:17–26). This teller seems to share the ancient assumption that whatever happens must be what LORD intended and, therefore, cannot deny that LORD consented to Saul's kingship, but wants to be sure we know that Israel's request was misguided and that LORD could have delivered without a king. The "Go Saul!" teller, however, resumes the deliverance story as soon as the interruption ends.

Saul enacts his role as deliverer in 1 Samuel 11. The coming of LORD's spirit upon Saul in 11:6 and the "dread of the LORD" which falls upon the people in 11:7 seem to indicate divine support for Saul, and in 11:13 Saul credits LORD for his victory. The one uneasy note here is the term "dread," which has a stronger supernatural connotation in Hebrew than in English but is just as negative in tone. LORD rouses the Israelites to follow Saul with a tool more commonly used to still Israel's enemies (Ex 15:16; Dt 2:25 and 11:25; and a number of other passages).

LORD and Samuel's Non-Farewell (1 Samuel 12)

Samuel's speech in 1 Samuel 12, like the shorter one in 10:17–19, reminds the people of all the good things LORD did for them prior to the monarchy and characterizes their request for a king as rebellion. This chapter, unlike 1 Samuel 8 and 10:17–19, contains no actual quotation (from the narrator or from the prophet) of LORD's words. I think the speech tells more about Samuel than about LORD, and so I will save most of my discussion of it for the next chapter. However, there is one striking piece of nonverbal input from LORD: "Samuel called upon the LORD, and the LORD sent thunder and rain that day; and all the people greatly feared the LORD and Samuel" (1 S 12:18). The storm, which occurs on the day of the wheat harvest, would likely result in loss of the year's crop, so this is not just an impressive sign but a significant blow. What we do not know is whether LORD agrees with Samuel's assessment that the people have acted wickedly and is punishing them accordingly or whether LORD is simply letting none of Samuel's words fall to the ground (see 3:19).

The people's response is fear: "all the people greatly feared the LORD and Samuel" (12:18). We often hear that the word "fear" in scripture really means "revere," but here I think it may really mean "fear" in the sense of being afraid. The phrasing of 12:18 intimates that the people identify LORD with Samuel. They beg Samuel to pray to "*your* [Samuel's] God," in contrast to their earlier request for Samuel to pray to "*our* God" (12:19 and 7:8, italics added). They also refer to themselves as "your [Samuel's] servants [*ʿăbādîm*]." This language is striking because the culminating argument of Samuel's warning against kingship in 1 Samuel 8 was, "you shall be his servants [*ʿăbādîm*]" (8:17, my translation; *ʿăbādîm* can be translated either "servants" or "slaves"). That the people describe themselves as Samuel's "servants" is also striking because Samuel has so emphasized that they should "serve" (*ʿbd*) only LORD (12:10, 14, 20, and 24). One might object that to serve Samuel is really the same as serving LORD. This is precisely what Samuel seems to want the people to believe—perhaps he believes it himself—and what the storytellers may want the audience to believe. In letting none of Samuel's words fall to the ground, LORD cooperates with a rhetoric that (like the rhetoric at the end of 1 Samuel 3) makes it difficult to distinguish the prophet from LORD. A question, of course, is whether this picture of LORD represents divine reality or the wish of prophetically oriented storytellers.

LORD Rejects and Replaces Saul (1 Samuel 13:1–16:13)

LORD's word remains rare (compare 3:3) in 1 Samuel 13–14. In 1 Samuel 13, Samuel says much about LORD's thoughts and feelings, but we get no confirming quotations of LORD's words by the narrator or by the prophet in the official messenger format. What we do get is a repeated accusation by Samuel that Saul has disobeyed *LORD's* commandment (13:13–14). But the commandment most obviously pertaining to the situation is the one *Samuel* gave in 10:8, "you shall go down to Gilgal ahead of me; then I will come down to you to present burnt offerings and offer sacrifices of well-being. Seven days you shall wait, until I come to you and show you what you shall do." Notice that even the narrator refers to the seven days as "the time appointed by Samuel" (13:8), not the "the time appointed by God." One does not need to be a formal biblical scholar to feel that something has gone awry here. If, according to the narrator, Samuel himself failed to fulfill his proposed plan ("but Samuel did not come," 13:8), why is Samuel so outraged that Saul has departed from it?

Fault on Saul's part is sufficiently unclear that interpreters sometimes go looking elsewhere to find the commandment. Not uncommonly I encounter the explanation that only prophets, not kings, are allowed to offer sacrifices. But as we saw earlier, in this period many different kinds of people offer sacrifices, and certainly other kings do so without censure (see, for example, 2 Samuel 6:13, where every six paces, "he [David] sacrificed an ox and a fatling," and 2 Samuel 24:25). When things get strict about sacrifice, it becomes a privilege of the priests (not prophets), and Samuel's lineage does not qualify him to be one of those priests.

David Toshio Tsumura, after reviewing the weaknesses of the various explanations about what commandment Saul violated, suggests that "it may be that Saul did not offend any specific commandment . . . but his lack of trust, going out for war without first seeking LORD's will through Samuel the prophet, was possibly the real issue here" (2007, 347). Later he remarks that Saul's "foolishness" (13:13) is primarily in "his failure to acknowledge the prophet's higher role as the divine messenger and to listen to the word of God" (348). I think he has put his finger on exactly what Samuel wants to convey, which is (as in chapter 12) Samuel's own indispensability as an interpreter of LORD's will. Tsumura does not, however, make any allowance for the possibility of a divergence between Samuel's assessment and LORD's, a divergence we know is possible from events such as Samuel's later exclamation that Jesse's eldest son, Eliab, is "surely the LORD's anointed" (16:6; LORD corrects Samuel in the next verse). At this point in the biblical text, we cannot know for sure whether LORD agrees with Samuel's assessment of Saul's action.

David Gunn, in *The Fate of King Saul,* also thinks the issue is Saul's acting without Samuel's instructions, although he refers here back to 10:8, suggesting that Saul has focused on "wait seven days" while Samuel takes "until I show you what you shall do" as more important. Gunn comments, "This instruction is ambiguous and . . . on Saul's understanding no sin has been committed. The question therefore resolves itself into one about the motives of Samuel and Yahweh. Why is no account taken of Saul's defence? Is Samuel unaware of the ambiguity of the instruction or does he *choose* to ignore it? Does the real cause of Saul's rejection lie, not in his action in chapter 13, but in the attitude of Yahweh toward him, or perhaps something he represents?" (1980, 40). He raises the possibility, also prominent in Eslinger's discussion, that Saul is held to an unreasonable standard because of LORD's ambivalence about kingship. Notice that Gunn, like Tsumura, supposes an essential solidarity between LORD and Samuel in chapter 13. On this supposition, Samuel's harshness and perhaps even unreasonableness reflect back onto LORD. But we have only Samuel's word to go on with regard to what LORD thinks, and Samuel is no disinterested player when it comes to Saul.

In 1 Samuel 14, LORD is again more talked about than talking. Saul's son Jonathan, having stated that "nothing can hinder the LORD from saving by many or by few," proposes a sign by which to judge whether he and his armor bearer have LORD's support for their exploit (14:6–9). The subsequent victory, accompanied by "panic" in the Philistine camp (a common signal of divine intervention in military matters) and an earthquake (14:15) suggests that Lord likes Jonathan's willingness to assume that "it may be that the Lord will act for us" (14:6). Saul's efforts are marked by three oaths (14:24, 39, and 44) and three inquiries into Lord's will, the first aborted, the second unanswered, and the third a lot casting that marks his son Jonathan for death (14:18–19, 36–37, and 40–45). Does Lord refuse to answer Saul's second request for advice out of pique because the earlier inquiry was aborted, or does Lord balk (as Saul assumes) because a sin has been committed? The lot's identification of Jonathan as offender might tilt us toward the latter opinion and might also suggest that Lord is working to end Saul's dynastic hopes (per Samuel's announcement in the previous chapter). Yet no obvious punishment falls upon the army or Saul when Jonathan is, in the end, ransomed. We remain uncertain about Lord's motives and level of involvement with Saul in this chapter.

In 1 Samuel 15, Lord takes an initiatory role for the third time in the book. (Prior to this, Lord took action against Eli's sons and sent Samuel to Saul; 1 S 2–3 and 9.) At the beginning of the chapter, in verses that technically come from Samuel's mouth but that I treat as Lord's own speech because they use an official messenger formula, Lord orders the complete destruction ("both man and woman, child and infant, ox and sheep, camel and donkey") of the desert tribe of Amalek (15:2–3). Lord, whose tendency to hold grudges is clearly in evidence, justifies the destruction as punishment for an Amalekite attack on Israel more than two hundred years earlier (Ex 17:8–16). Saul does defeat Amalek, but he warns away the Kenites (traditional allies of Israel) and spares the Amalekite king and some of the livestock.

Lord then speaks directly in 15:10 to say that he regrets (using the same Hebrew term that is translated in 15:29 as "change his mind") having chosen Saul—a sentiment confirmed by the narrator's statement in 15:35. While most people think of God as omniscient and assume that God knows in advance how events will turn out, it appears, from the contrast between Lord's confident designation of Saul as deliverer in 9:16–17 and Lord's regret in the present chapter, that Lord did not quite anticipate how things would go with Saul.

Just what command has Saul failed to carry out this time? Gunn argues that here, as in 1 Samuel 13, Saul is caught in a controversy over interpretation rather than in flat-out disobedience (1980, 45–55). The interpretive point at issue, in Gunn's view, is whether the utter destruction commanded in 15:3 needs to carried out at the scene of battle. According to Gunn, Saul might reasonably have thought that the command could be fulfilled by killing most of the captured livestock on the battlefield but bringing the rest, the best, to Gilgal for formal sacrifice. He says that if Saul had intended to keep the livestock for himself, he would never have brought the animals to the sacred assembly site of Gilgal, where Saul could expect to encounter Samuel.

In 1 Samuel 13 we were not sure whether Lord agreed with Samuel's interpretation of the situation. Here Lord is shown expressing an opinion. Gunn, whom we have already seen questioning Lord's motives in 1 Samuel 13, has this to say: "If we are to condemn Saul for his jealous persecution of David, how much more is Yahweh to be condemned for his jealous persecution of Saul!" "Yahweh manipulates Saul mercilessly," says Gunn, "and he does so for what, on most people's terms, must count as less than honourable motives. He is insulted, feels jealous, is anxious to justify himself. . . . We might say that here we see the dark side of God" (1984, 129). At the very least, Lord is here characterized—again—as someone demanding absolute obedience to commandments conveyed by a prophet and as someone quite willing to revoke a prior commitment to a leader (we saw this already in 2:30), in contradiction to Samuel's assertion in 15:29 that "the Glory of Israel will not recant or change his mind."

Lord continues to initiate action with the instruction in 16:1 for Samuel to go to Bethlehem. In 8:7 Lord issued a mild correction to Samuel ("listen to the voice of the people . . . for they have not rejected you, but they have rejected me"), and 15:11 intimates that Samuel made requests that Lord refused, but in 16:1 Lord's impatience with Samuel seems to have sharpened. "How long you will grieve? . . . Fill your horn with oil and set out." Another reprimand comes in 16:7: "Do not look on his appearance . . . because I have rejected him." Following the anointing, the Lord who brings low and also exalts (2:7) not only withdraws spirit from Saul and sends it upon David, but additionally sends an evil spirit to torment Saul (16:13–14).[16] Once again Lord shows a capacity for destructive action.

Samuel insists in the Hebrew text of 15:29 that "the Glory of Israel will not deceive" (NRSV note). However, we have already seen Lord prevaricate about whether Eli took action on the problem with his sons (3:13 and 2:22–25). Lord's willingness to mislead is evident again in 16:3 when Lord tells Samuel to "say, 'I have come to sacrifice.'" It is true that Samuel will offer a sacrifice, but Lord is having him deceive the elders of Bethlehem about the real purpose of his visit, the anointing of a new king-designate. Lord seems to misrepresent affairs yet again in chiding Samuel for his incorrect identification of Eliab as the anointed: "Do not look on his appearance . . . for the Lord does not see as mortals see; they look on the outward appearance, but the Lord looks on the heart" (16:7). If, as most commentators believe, the remark pertains not only to Eliab but to the similarly tall and good-looking Saul (see 9:2 and 10:3), Lord's implication is that only mortals, who do not see the heart, would ever have made such a mistaken choice. But both 9:16–17 and 10:20–24 hold Lord, not mortals, responsible for the selection of

Saul. Furthermore, according to the notice in 10:9 about LORD giving Saul "another heart," if there were problems with Saul's heart, LORD was responsible for them. To complete the irony, when we finally meet LORD's new choice, David, he also turns out to be unusually good looking (16:12). But why is LORD so touchy? Jobling suggests that "throughout the whole anointing scene YHWH pays Samuel back, in a childish and self-contradictory way, for his reluctance [to anoint another king]." "What we have here," says Jobling, "is another example of YHWH becoming irrational about the choosing of kings and Samuel taking the blame" (1998, 84).

Coda (Selected Incidents from the Rest of 1 Samuel)

Once David is anointed, we no longer see LORD interacting with Samuel. Historically I suspect this is because Samuel's career did not actually overlap with David's (I rather doubt that Samuel even anointed David), but narratively it leaves the impression that LORD is far more interested in David than in Samuel. Samuel makes just one more appearance while alive, when David flees to him in 19:18–24 and LORD's spirit sends the pursuing Saul into a naked frenzy—yet another instance in which LORD's intervention is more destructive than constructive.

In 1 Samuel 28, LORD for the last time refuses to answer Saul's pleas for advice (28:6). Samuel, whose ghost does supply Saul with some commentary, speaks of LORD as one whose anger is implacable against the king who failed so long ago to be an adequate agent of LORD's "fierce wrath." While we may believe that we should approve of Saul's removal, what are we to think about LORD handing Saul's sons and the army of Israel over to the Philistines in the process (28:19; with the prediction fulfilled in 1 Samuel 31)? What an irony that while Saul is dying, David battles the Amalekites (a battle from which four hundred of their fighting men escape) and presents his loot to the elders of Judah, who will soon crown him king (1 S 30:16–20 and 26–29; 2 S 2:4). Contrast this to Saul's punishment for not destroying all Amalekites and their loot in 1 Samuel 15. This LORD's ways are neither gentle nor consistent.

REFLECTIONS

While many modern monotheists understand love to be a primary characteristic of God, in 1 Samuel it is only human characters who show love to one another.[17] In this book no human is ever said to love LORD, nor is LORD ever said to love a human, although Jonathan attributes "faithful love" (*ḥesed,* a term denoting loyalty or favor usually from a social superior to an inferior) to LORD in 1 Samuel 20:14. LORD also shows little interest in social justice. For all Hannah's ebullient praise of LORD as one who raises up the poor to sit with princes, the only help we see LORD giving to the poor is military protection, and those stories of military deliverance must be weighed against ones in which LORD's displeasure with leaders prompts the handing over of Israel to defeat by the Philistines. Even in dealing with chosen leaders, LORD is often harsh. Eli is cast off despite his efforts to correct his sons, Samuel and LORD both seem determined to find fault with Saul, and even David comes to the throne only after years of divinely inspired (according to 1 Samuel) persecution by Saul. The primary motive for serving LORD in 1 Samuel seems to be fear: fear of enemies who may overwhelm Israel if it does not have LORD's protection and fear of LORD's own reprisals if obedience is not absolute.

Christians sometimes describe the God of the books of Samuel as an Old Testament (or Jewish) "God of wrath," in contrast to a New Testament (or Christian) "God of love." While Samuel's LORD does seem to be a "God of wrath," I think it is wrong to set this up as an Old Testament / New Testament distinction, much less a Jewish/Christian one. What is really at stake, I think, is the difference between Axial (and post-Axial) ideas of God and the pre-Axial traditions to which they are still connected.

I am drawing here on an idea developed by a German psychiatrist and philosopher, Karl Jaspers, who described the period in and around the fifth century (400s) B.C.E. as a pivotal, or "axial," age in which religious genius flourished across Europe and Asia (Jaspers 1953). Great religious and spiritual movements originating in the Axial Age include biblical Judaism (in which today's Judaism, Christianity, and Islam are all rooted), classical Greek philosophy, Buddhism, classical Hinduism, Confucianism, Taoism, and Zoroastrianism. Jaspers's work has fallen somewhat by the wayside, partly because contemporary scholarship suggests that the people and movements he discusses were spread across a wider time period than he realized, but even more because scholarship in recent decades has emphasized the uniqueness of particular cultures and been relatively reluctant to speak of wider patterns of historical development. However, the religious developments of the mid–first millennium B.C.E. remain remarkable, and the idea of an Axial Age seems to be attracting renewed interest.[18]

To put things simply, pre-Axial thought attributes events such as childlessness, disease, earthquakes, thunderstorms, and military defeats to spirit powers. The point of religion is then to avert disaster and attain health, wealth, and long life by magically manipulating the spirit powers (if they are thought of in impersonal terms) or winning their favor (if they are thought of in personal terms). The powers themselves are not regarded as being particularly moral or predictable—they cannot be, given the unpredictability and lack of moral consistency in the events being attributed to them. The Samuel narratives seem to have just such a sensibility. They understand barrenness, plague, and military defeat as divine actions. For early Israel the events of life were often quite harsh, so LORD comes across harshly, too.

In the Axial Age, the inhabitants of a wide swath of the globe begin to ask a new and different set of questions. Instead of just asking how to get health, wealth, and prestige, they begin asking whether there might be more to life than that. Instead of only trying to teach people to do what society expects of them, wise teachers begin to ponder what society *ought* to expect of its members, and whether there might be circumstances in which an individual should resist society's demands. Axial religious and philosophical systems demand personal commitment, whereas pre-Axial beliefs and practices had been part of the world one was born into. Today we take the questions and premises of Axial religion for granted (although we are, perhaps, not much beyond the ancients in answering the questions and living out those answers). However, such ideas have not always been part of human life or religion.

I think the book of Deuteronomy is moving toward an Axial outlook, and certainly the finished Hebrew Bible has such a sensibility. But while religions do, over time, pick up new ideas and images, they seldom leave behind the old ones. One reason for not characterizing the God of wrath / God of love distinction as an Old Testament / New Testament or Jewish/Christian one is that many parts of the Old Testament and certainly Judaism have much to say about a God of love. A second reason is that the New Testament and Christianity have not left the God of wrath behind. If you doubt me, read the book of Revelation.[19]

The Axial Age seems to have left little imprint on the books of Samuel, even though the most recent editorial layers come from the dawn of that age in Israel. The Samuel stories portray LORD as a war god with a touchy ego. LORD sometimes acts in ways that turn out well for the people but may also send a thunderstorm to destroy the year's wheat harvest as a warning against disobedience that has not occurred. LORD may or may not have plans to save the oppressed but can certainly be expected to punish disrespect. In the later parts of the books of Samuel, LORD does show strong support for David and Solomon. That favor, however, continues the patterns we have already seen: its expressions have little to do with fairness, ethics, or the people's well-being.[20]

CHAPTER 5

A SEQUENTIAL READING OF SAMUEL

Chapters 2 through 4 examined some probable layers in the composition of the book of 1 Samuel, the roles commonly ascribed to the character Samuel, and how God is depicted in the Samuel stories. With this as background, we turn at last to the most obvious strategy for understanding Samuel: a sequential journey through his story. Three themes are worthy of particular attention: the relationship of Samuel's word to LORD's, the question of who (if anyone) can intercede with LORD, and points at which there is tension between Samuel and LORD. Earlier I mentioned students of mine who had compared Samuel to very powerful pastors. Like those students, I want to approach Samuel with both a "hermeneutic of suspicion" and a "hermeneutic of charity."[1] On the one hand, what power games are Samuel and the storytellers who present him to us playing, and how do those games affect other people? On the other, what positive purposes do Samuel and the tellers have in mind, and how might all this feel to the Samuel we meet in the story?

SAMUEL'S EARLIEST YEARS (1 SAMUEL 1–2)

Samuel comes, it appears, from a troubled family. His father has two wives, and they do not get along well together. It would be inappropriate to attempt too detailed a speculation on the family dynamics from the very limited information we get in 1 Samuel 1, but Elkanah may be contributing to the strife between his wives by favoritism, if he is indeed giving Hannah a double portion (1:5, but as NRSV's note indicates, the meaning here is uncertain). Polzin hears a tone of "loving understanding" in Elkanah's words to Hannah (1:8; 1989, 23), but one could also hear impatience (Fewell and Gunn 1993, 137). Elkanah's focus is not on Hannah's grief but on questioning her love for him: "Am I not more to you than ten sons?" (1:8; Falk 1994, 62). If these commentators are correct that Elkanah sounds a bit narcissistic, then Polzin's contention that Elkanah's tone prefigures God's (1:8 and 8:8) implies a different conclusion than the one Polzin himself draws (1989, 86).

While children were important in the ancient world in part because their parents depended on them for care in old age, the emphasis in 1 Samuel 1 on rivalry between the wives suggests that for Hannah the issue is status, not simply survival. Jobling asks if she might be an "ambitious woman" who "wants . . . a son *in the service of YHWH*" (1998, 132, Jobling's italics). Whatever Hannah's reasons for wanting a child, they do not include keeping him, and they do include establishing certain constraints for his life before he is even born: no razor, probably no alcoholic beverages, and "given to the LORD."[2]

Hannah delivers the child to Eli as soon as he is weaned. Children typically nurse longer in agrarian cultures than in our own, so Samuel is probably about three years old when he is brought to Eli—the same age as the bull that his parents slaughter (1:24–25).[3] While this is beyond the crucial period for attachment formation, it is nonetheless a very early age for a child to leave his own family to live with a stranger in a different town. For all our desire to attribute piety to Samuel, can we really believe that at this young age he wants to leave his family to serve LORD? Surely he asks, "Why do you have to leave me at Shiloh?" Hannah presumably answers, "Because that is what I vowed to do." "Why do you have to keep the vow?" "Because LORD will not tolerate turning back."

What kind of world does this establish for Samuel? If he has been told the circumstances of his own remarkable birth, he may have a special sense of importance and destiny. But if the story told to him has included the family's belief that it was LORD who initially prevented Hannah from having a child, Samuel may also feel that his existence is precarious, dependent on a not-always-benevolent power. It will also be apparent to the young Samuel as he is taken to Shiloh that LORD's demands upon devotees take priority over even the most fundamental human relationships. How does he feel when his mother's parting prayer ends with praise for LORD's thundering support of "his king" (who does not yet exist), with not a word about Samuel himself?[4]

This is, of course, a story. Quite naturally we imagine the events unfolding in an actual life—whether the story tells of an actual historical life or whether it reports its events accurately. This is how we are supposed to react to stories, and this is why I feel entitled to ask how Samuel feels about being given away. Yet we have a quite peculiar perspective on that imagined world. Years of the imagined Samuel's life are reduced for us to the brief notice in 2:19 that Hannah takes him a handmade robe when she visits Shiloh each year. We also have information that may not be available to characters in the story.[5] For instance, we know why Eli's sons have disregarded his warning ("it was the will of the LORD to kill them"; 2:25), while Samuel does not (except perhaps as a deduction from general theological principle). We hear Hannah's song with Judges 21:25 ringing in our ears: "in those days there was no king in Israel; all the people did what was right in their own eyes." But this sentence, enunciated by a storyteller later in time (note the phrase "in those days") does not exist in Hannah's world.

The audience of 1 Samuel 2 learns much about the sins of Eli's sons, Eli's attempt to correct them, and God's plans concerning them. The chapter does not tell us what Samuel knows about these matters. Almost certainly he knows something is awry (especially if he has the duties of the *na'ar* mentioned in 2:13–16). It seems less certain that he would have witnessed Eli's rebuke, and less likely still that he would have heard the prophecy of the man of God. But we the audience know these things, and they raise questions about who will speak for God, who can intercede with God, and what happens to people who do not please God.

SAMUEL'S CALLING (1 SAMUEL 3:1–4:1)

Our imagined Samuel's nighttime encounter with LORD is surely a pivotal experience in his life. Samuel, who "did not yet know the LORD" (3:7; presumably because word and visions of LORD have been rare [3:1]), initially cannot tell the difference between LORD's voice and Eli's. Eli, however, correctly discerns the caller's identity and instructs Samuel about how to respond (3:9). Samuel follows Eli's instructions closely but not exactly, dropping the word "LORD" (3:10). Is he hedging his bets because he is not quite sure he believes Eli about the caller's identity?

The message Samuel receives is certainly enough to make his ears tingle and confirm whatever suspicions he may already have about LORD's implacability. LORD announces that the sins of Eli's sons "shall not be expiated by sacrifice or offering forever" (3:14). Regardless of whether Eli has told Samuel his doubts about the possibility of intercession for those who sin against LORD (2:25), LORD's words and Eli's resigned reaction to them (3:18) confirm for Samuel that there can be no appeal of LORD's verdicts.

Why is Samuel "afraid to tell the vision to Eli" (3:15)? We need to be careful here to differentiate between what we guess, based on our imagining of the story world, and what we actually know. Eli's "my son" language (3:6) suggests that the relationship between Eli and his fosterling is an affectionate one (although this is also traditional teacher/pupil language). If the relationship is affectionate, Samuel probably does not want to be the bearer of hurtful news. Samuel might also fear Eli's anger, although we have no reason to suspect Eli of an explosive temper: it is not evident in his pleading with his sons, and when he does receive Samuel's report, he reacts quietly. What we do know with certainty is that in his very first commission from LORD, Samuel is not eager to deliver the message.

After this initial encounter, LORD continues to be with Samuel and appears and speaks to him at Shiloh (3:19–4:1). Samuel accordingly becomes known "from Dan to Beersheba" as a "trustworthy prophet." Twice in four verses the narrator speaks of Samuel's ministry to "all Israel." I noted earlier that the phrasing of this report emphasizes Samuel's word, not simply LORD's: "the LORD was with him and let none of his [Samuel's?!] words fall to the ground," and "the word of *Samuel* came to all Israel" (3:19 and 4:1, italics added). Possibly the emphasis on Samuel is meant to underscore that the era of Eli and his family, who remain unmentioned, is passing. However, I suggest that the phrasing also reveals a narrator who, consciously or unconsciously, does not distinguish between Samuel's word and Lord's (compare Samuel's earlier confusion about Eli's words and Lord's). The narrator may even be deliberately encouraging us to equate Samuel's word with Lord's. It remains to be seen if Samuel is aware of a possible difference between them.

INTERLUDE OF ABSENCE (1 SAMUEL 4:2–7:2)

The timeline implied by the notice of Samuel's prophetic status in 3:19–4:1 suggests a period during which Samuel grows up and prophesies while Eli's family continues to minister at the altar. We have no stories, however, depicting such an overlap. Eli is not mentioned in the description of Samuel's establishment, and Samuel is nowhere in sight as Eli and his sons die in 1 Samuel 4. Indeed, after the first sentence of 4:1, Samuel appears not at all in 1 Samuel 4–6. I suspect that Samuel's absence is due not, in the first instance, to deliberate narrative artistry, but to the editors' use here of a different source (often referred to as the "ark narrative") that did not include Samuel.[6] One might suppose that Samuel, established as a prophet, advised the Israelites that their battle plans were unwise, but if so, they ignored his advice. As the story is now presented, Eli's downfall establishes Samuel's legitimacy as an announcer of divine rejection, while Samuel's absence from the ark narrative frees him from any taint of association with defeat.

SAMUEL AS JUDGE (1 SAMUEL 7:3–17)

In 1 Samuel 7, Samuel emerges as a strong leader, powerfully supported by God. The people immediately follow his appeal to "put away the foreign gods and the Astartes" (showing, perhaps, how the writers think people ought to respond to prophetic exhortations). Then Samuel gathers the Israelites at Mizpah, where he says he will "pray" to Lord for them. This is a striking and important statement, for the verb that NRSV here translates "pray" is the same verb and stem that is translated "make intercession" in 2:25 ("if someone sins against the Lord, who can make intercession?"). Until now, all the evidence has supported Eli's statement that there can be no intercession for sins against Lord, but here Samuel takes it upon himself to make just such intercession.

It is preceded, to be sure, by the people's obedient gathering, fasting, and confession.[7] Samuel's first response is not to "intercede/pray" for them, but to "judge" (*špṭ*) them, and we are left to wonder whether this is "judging" in a judicial or a governing sense. The former seems more likely, since it seems to be a single event at Mizpah.

The Philistines (apparently uncowed by their experience with the ark) muster to attack the gathered Israelites, and the frightened people beg Samuel, "do not cease to cry out . . . for us, and pray that he may save us" (7:8). While the Hebrew contains no word corresponding to NRSV's "pray" (its construction is closer to NJB's "Do not stop calling on Yahweh our God to rescue us"), the idea of intercession is certainly present. Samuel accordingly makes a burnt offering, cries out, and is answered (7:10–11) by thunder and the confusion and routing of the Philistines.[8]

Following this initial victory, Samuel establishes a circuit to "judge" (*špṭ*) the people at Bethel, Gilgal, and Mizpah. Again the word "judge" could be narrowly judicial in implication or denote a wider governing role. The similarities of this chapter to the stories in Judges (military victory followed by peace "all the days" of the leader) favor the wider governing sense, which appears again in the people's request for a king (8:5).

Taking *špṭ* in a more restricted judicial sense might square the notice in 7:15 that "Samuel judged Israel all the days of his life" more easily with the overlap between Samuel's life and Saul's reign as king.[9] However, alongside that notice of Samuel's lifelong judging, 7:13–14 claims that the Philistines did not again enter Israel's territory and that they even returned already captured towns "from Ekron to Gath" during "all the days of Samuel." This description of the situation is contradicted by other material in 1 Samuel. LORD's words in 9:16 ("he [Saul] shall save my people from the hand of the Philistines") already acknowledge an ongoing Philistine problem, and in 1 Samuel 14 the Philistines have a garrison in Israelite territory. In other words there are more problems with the ending of 1 Samuel 7 than just its claim that Samuel judged/governed all the days of his life.

How do we process such inconsistency? Many people simply do not notice it. But once noticed, it affects our reading. No longer do the narrator's words seem a transparent window into the world of the story. A "frame break" occurs; our attention shifts to the act of telling rather than resting with what is being told about.[10]

In the previous chapter, I suggested imagining that we hear the Samuel stories from a sequence of tellers. I imagine the teller of 1 Samuel 7 as quite old, although not nearly old enough to have lived through any of these events. He is dismayed by the troubles he has seen his people and their leaders get themselves into. Surely we could do better, he believes. If we just had a leader who really knew God's will and if we would just do what that leader asked, surely God would deliver us from our troubles. Was it not like that back when Samuel ruled? Let me tell you how it was, he says. Why cannot we do it now?

One can empathize with this teller's longing for a world in which there is no doubt about who speaks for God, all the people respond appropriately, and God eliminates their problems. After this teller's "happily ever after," we expect to hear about Samuel's death, in line with the pattern established in the book of Judges. (The same expectation arises at the end of 1 Samuel 12.)[11] But this teller is only one in a series. Others remember that it was not that simple. There were problems even in Samuel's day, and not all of them were the people's fault. They lived happily ever after, until. . . . "Until . . ." takes us into 1 Samuel 8.

REQUEST FOR KINGSHIP (1 SAMUEL 8)

Why, at the beginning of 1 Samuel 8, does Samuel appoint his sons judges? Does he not know them well enough to know that they will take advantage of the situation? Has he forgotten LORD's response to the corruption of Eli's sons? How can Samuel, experienced by many as the Bible's most powerful spokesperson against kingship, be himself introducing a "dynastic principle" into Israel's governance (8:1–2; Fokkelman 1993, 326)?[12] Jobling finds the characterization of Samuel at this point absurd: "The greatest of judges, at the moment of triumph for him and his office, so far forgets the nature of judgeship as to try to make it hereditary" (1998, 63).[13]

Whatever Samuel's reasons, his action creates a genuine problem for the elders of Israel (8:3–5). Samuel *is* old and his sons do *not* follow in his ways, and the people may very well fear more defeats, like those of 1 Samuel 4, should LORD decide to punish the sons (Eslinger 1985, 255). That the elders do come to Samuel shows their continuing respect for him. They, like the narrator and possibly Samuel himself, may still regard the "word of Samuel" as the functional equivalent of LORD's word.

Samuel is displeased by their request. How much of Samuel's opposition to kingship comes from a sense that it violates egalitarian Israelite ideals (Jobling 1998, 73–74) and how much from dismay at rejection of his own leadership? We can easily imagine that the trajectory depicted in 1 Samuel 7 would leave Samuel with a secure sense of his own role as divinely appointed leader. He has successfully called the nation to repentance and even managed an intercession of the kind that Eli doubted possible. In response to his prayers LORD has intervened against the Philistines, reversing the woeful military situation of 1 Samuel 4–6. And LORD has not, so far as we know, made any proactive moves to provide new leadership in the face of Samuel's aging. Would it be surprising if Samuel got a bit overconfident about LORD's and the people's support for his decisions, as David also seems to do at one point in his career?[14]

While the reason for Samuel's displeasure is not directly stated, LORD's response to it suggests that Samuel complains about being personally rejected (8:6–7, over against the assertion by many preachers that Samuel is upset by the elders' rejection of *God*). Earlier I reviewed some proposals about the tone of LORD's response. Polzin finds LORD "predominantly disinterested and remarkably magnanimous" and Samuel, by contrast, "full of self-interest," "trying to delay or subvert the LORD's command" (Polzin 1989, 87). Peter Miscall, on the other hand, claims that

LORD "gives no evaluation of the request or of a king; he is directing and supporting Samuel, his judge and prophet" (1986, 49; Miscall believes that in 8:7–8 LORD refers to past rejections, not the present request).

I adopted Miscall's reading in a 2002 paper entitled "Looking for a Friend," arguing that LORD sees in Samuel a friend with whom to commiserate about the ungratefulness of the people. Now, however, I am more inclined to hear LORD's words to Samuel as a rebuke. "How can you worry about being rejected when they are rejecting *me*? How dare you be upset about it when *I* have been putting up with it since Egypt?" This is consistent with LORD's pattern of touchiness about disrespect and with the fact that nowhere else does LORD show any particular concern for Samuel's feelings. In this interpretation LORD's inconsistency with regard to whether Samuel is being rejected (8:7–8) shows that LORD is not really interested in Samuel's problem. LORD is interested in whether the people are rejecting LORD, on which point the two verses agree. LORD's instruction to Samuel to "listen to their voice" (8:7, 9, and 22) might then be a punishment not only of the people, but of Samuel for daring to be upset on his own behalf.

It is not clear whether Samuel's lecture on the evils of kingship (8:11–18) fulfills LORD's command to "show them the ways of the king" (8:9, with the caution that we do not know whether these verses contain the whole of what Samuel said). Polzin observes that the theme of kingship as a rejection of LORD is conspicuously absent from the quoted speech, although surely a prophet ought to bring this issue to the people's attention (1985, 82, 84–88). Instead Samuel focuses on the material disadvantages of kingship. For Polzin (who does not see LORD's granting of kingship as vengeful), Samuel's effort to talk the people out of it is "shrewdly self-serving" (87).

Eslinger, by contrast, contests translations (such as NRSV) in which LORD asks Samuel to "solemnly warn" and "show" (8:9). Eslinger believes that LORD orders Samuel to "stipulate" and "declare" how kings should act, setting forth appropriate constraints on royal action (1985, 268–70; which references Veijola 1977, 64). If so, this chapter has LORD giving a prophet authority over kings, an idea we encounter again in the stories of Samuel's interactions with Saul. Samuel's eventual writing up of "the rights and duties of the kingship" (the word translated "rights" in 1 Samuel 10:25 is the same one that NRSV renders "ways" in 1 Samuel 8:9) may then be his fulfilling of this order.

In 1 Samuel 8, Samuel does not design a program for kingship but tries to talk the people out of it. "Yahweh tells Samuel to *prescribe* 'the manner'; instead Samuel *describes* it" (1985, 271, Eslinger's italics). Eslinger, like Polzin, thinks Samuel's speech defends Samuel's own interests. "Ironically, it is the very fear of losing his role as mediator that prevents Samuel from fulfilling that role" (271–72).

Samuel's description of kingship is noticeably one sided. The people have spoken of their need for military leadership ("go out before us and fight our battles" [8:20], as both Saul and David will do). Samuel says nothing of it, nor of the king's role in governing / maintaining justice (*špṭ*, from which the term *mišpāṭ* "duties/ways/rights" comes). Samuel focuses only on the king's *taking*.

Is Samuel driven only by fear of losing his own job? Perhaps he also fears for the people. Samuel's early experiences with Lord (1 S 1 and 3) have been unpleasant, and the events of 1 Samuel 4–6 would give him further reason to fear God. Things seem to have gone well during Samuel's judgeship (1 S 7), but he has just been reminded again of how touchy Lord's ego is. However valid the people's concerns about governance and military protection, the dangers of a plan that Lord experiences as rejection may, in Samuel's eyes, be even greater: recall the defeats of 1 Samuel 4 and the smiting of the Beth-shemeshites in 1 Samuel 6:19. Although in 1 Samuel 7, Samuel cried out to Lord and got an answer, he now paints a scenario in which there can be no intercession: "In that day you will cry out . . . but the Lord will not answer" (8:18).

Three times in 1 Samuel 8, Lord tells Samuel to obey the people (verses 7, 9, 22), but at the end of the chapter, Samuel tells them, "each of you return home." Like Hannah, who wanted to keep her child at least until he was weaned (1:22–23), Samuel delays. It is not a flagrantly disobedient delay, not beyond the bounds of reason, but it does suggest reluctance. As in 3:15, where Samuel was afraid to tell his vision to Eli, and 8:6–9, where Samuel and God spar over the elders' request, in 8:22 we get a hint that Samuel may not always agree with Lord's outlook and plans.

SAMUEL DESIGNATES SAUL (1 SAMUEL 9:1–10:27)

We have seen that 1 Samuel 9:1–10:16 presents kingship in a surprisingly positive light. Here even Lord seems to approve, speaking of Saul in terms reminiscent of the book of Judges: "he shall save my people from the hand of the Philistines."[15] Samuel appears in this story less as a judge or even national prophet than as a local holy man who can tell people where to find lost items and expects to be paid for doing so (9:7–8).

While an earlier version of this story may have featured an anonymous seer, in the present version the seer is Samuel. Saul's servant describes him as a "man held in honor," adding that "whatever he says always comes true" (9:6). Samuel does correctly answer Saul's question about the donkeys (9:20, compare 10:2 and 9), and we know that Samuel's words to Saul in 10:1 are true because we have heard Lord give Samuel the information in 9:15–17. Samuel's authority is evident as he orders Saul about: "go up before me," "give no further thought," "eat," "get up," "tell the boy . . . stop here yourself" (9:19, 20, 24, 26, and 27). The orders culminate in the potentially conflicting instructions in 10:7–8 to "do whatever you see fit" and "wait." The instruction for Saul to wait at Gilgal is preceded by images of the townspeople waiting for Samuel (9:13) and Saul waiting the night at Samuel's instruction. Samuel, it seems, is someone that people wait for.

Saul is hardly granted unbridled power. The signs outlined by Samuel (10:9–12) may confirm Saul's authority ("This shall be the sign to you that the Lord has anointed you ruler over his heritage. . . . When these signs meet you, do whatever you see fit to do, for God is with you," 10:1 and 7), but their fulfillment also underscores Samuel's authority. The fulfillments lend weight to his command, "Wait, until I come to you and show you what you shall do" (10:8). Saul's prophetic frenzy (9:10–13) has a similarly ambiguous quality for the king-designate. As part of the sign-fulfillment series it seems to validate his new status, but his possession by "the spirit of God" does not appear to inspire confidence in those who see him. Perhaps this foreshadows the ongoing problems that Samuel's power will create for Saul.

In 1 Samuel 10:17–27, Samuel again takes command—if he ever let go of it. He summons the people to Mizpah, lectures them again on the mistake they have made in asking for a king, presides over the choosing of a king by lot, declares "the rights and duties of the kingship" (10:25), and then dismisses the people to their homes. Samuel even, like Moses, writes up his declarations in a book. Saul never speaks a word and goes home with the rest—hardly a decisive beginning for his reign.

Since the people have already recognized Samuel's authority to appoint a king (8:5) and Lord has already identified his chosen candidate to Samuel, why must lots be cast? I noted earlier that the language of this scene is strikingly passive: Benjamin, Kish, and finally Saul "were taken by lot" (10:20–21), but we do not know who cast the lots. I suggest that the narrator's passive language distances Samuel from the choice, as does Samuel's own rhetoric, which makes Saul the people's choice ("you have said, 'No! but set a king over us,'" 10:19) and Lord's ("the one whom the Lord has chosen"), but not necessarily Samuel's.

In this respect I disagree with Jobling, who thinks that Samuel's words in 10:24 "could scarcely express greater enthusiasm for Saul" (1998, 120). Jobling even plays with the notion of a master/apprentice relationship between Samuel and Saul, which might be implied by Samuel's words in 10:8 and the subsequent induction of Saul into the prophetic band. But in connection with this idea Jobling also points out Samuel's words in 12:23, "I will instruct you [Israel] in the good and right way," and asks, "how better to exercise this function than as advisor to the new king?" (1998, 120). It is a good question. We do not see Samuel acting as adviser. In 10:25 Samuel instructs *the people* about the rights and duties of the kingship. But when Samuel sends everyone home, Saul goes too. He does not remain with Samuel for further tutelage, nor does Samuel follow Saul.

SAUL STEPS FORWARD (1 SAMUEL 11)

Samuel does little in connection with the Nahash incident of 1 Samuel 11 (Saul's judgelike inauguration into military leadership). It is easy to imagine that an earlier version of the chapter did not include him, since all three mentions of him look suspiciously like insertions. Saul's words, "whoever does not come out after Saul and Samuel" (11:7), imply Samuel's presence at the battle, but the narrator does not confirm that presence. When the fighting is done, the people ask Samuel, "Who is it that said, 'shall Saul reign over us?'" (11:12; notice that Saul, not Samuel, responds). Most interpreters suppose that the people are referring to the "worthless fellows" of 10:27, but in the present version they put their question to a prophet who himself has shown (if I am right, rather than Jobling) no great enthusiasm for Saul.

Samuel then proposes a trip to Gilgal to renew (or, with TNK, "inaugurate") the kingship. But at Gilgal it is the people ("they," 11:15) who make Saul king, and it is "Saul and all the Israelites" who rejoice greatly. Samuel is conspicuous by his absence in this rejoicing.

SAMUEL'S FAREWELL SPEECH? (1 SAMUEL 12)

Samuel's distancing of himself from the king in 1 Samuel 10–11 gives way to open condemnation of kingship in 1 Samuel 12, often referred to as Samuel's "farewell address." His sense of personal pique is apparent in his demand that the people testify to his honesty in leadership. In 12:2 he mentions both his age and his sons, as the elders did in their request for a king (8:5), but without any mention of the sons' corruption (which we have, in fact, never seen Samuel acknowledge or try to correct). Later in the speech, he says that the people's request for a king was motivated by fear of King Nahash (Saul's opponent in 1 Samuel 11). Historically this may simply be a different tradition than the one behind 1 Samuel 8. Literarily, however, the narrator's version of events establishes our baseline, with respect to which Samuel's memory is both selective (overlooking his sons' corruption) and distorted (confusing the order in which the kingship request and Nahash's oppression occur). Samuel's slips of memory are humanly understandable. What father wants to remember his sons' failures? What leader wants to remember that he was asked to appoint a replacement for himself? But with such humanly understandable foibles in evidence, we should refrain from speaking as if Samuel's viewpoints can be simply equated with LORD's.

A more subtle discrepancy between chapters 8 and 12 appears in the opening line of Samuel's speech. In 1 Samuel 8, Lord orders Samuel to "listen to their [the people's] voice" and "set a king over them" (8:22). In 12:1, Samuel reports an *almost* exact fulfilling of those orders. He uses the same idiom of "listening to the voice" (although this cannot be seen in NRSV's translation, which folds the Hebrew word "voice" into the verb "listened" in 12:1), with the "all" from 8:5 and 7 and the expression "make a king be king" that appears in 8:22 (NRSV streamlines this into the less redundant English expression "set a king"). However, in 8:22 Lord instructs Samuel to make a king *for* them (Hebrew *lāhem*). In Samuel's farewell speech, this becomes a king *over* the people (Hebrew *ʿălêkem*; Dhorme 1910, 100). The subtle change presages the strong antikingship position Samuel will take in this speech.

The remainder of the speech (12:6–25) is reminiscent of Moses's farewell in Deuteronomy and Joshua's in Joshua 24.[16] This is not the first time we have noted parallels among Moses, Joshua, and Samuel. The speech rehearses Lord's saving actions from the exodus to the time of Samuel, with a special emphasis on the requirement that Israel put aside foreign deities and worship Lord alone (12:6–13; compare Josh 24:2–13). Samuel warns of dire consequences if the people disobey Lord (12:14–15; compare Josh 24:14–23).

Samuel finishes with a dramatic sign and some remarkable rhetorical maneuvering. I have already spoken about the destructiveness of the sign Samuel chooses (a thunderstorm on the day of the wheat harvest) and the uncertainty about whether Lord shares Samuel's opinion of the request for a king or is simply "letting none of Samuel's words fall to the ground." Once the thunderstorm comes, however, the people forget whatever fears may originally have inspired their request for a king. Instead, the narrator tells us, "all the people greatly feared the Lord and Samuel."

The people's response reprises the theme of intercession, as they beg Samuel to "pray" for them (1 S 12:19; same Hebrew vocabulary as 7:5 and 2:25). But earlier the people said, "do not cease to cry out to the Lord *our* God for us" (7:8, italics added). Now, as we have seen, they plead for Samuel to "pray to the Lord *your* God for your servants" (12:19, italics added). One might regard the shift from "our God" to "your God" as inconsequential, did not so much else in this chapter also work to position Samuel with Lord in contrast to the people ("all the people greatly feared the Lord and Samuel").

It is also worth noticing once again that in 8:17, Samuel warned the people that they would become their king's "servants" (*ʿăbādîm*, NRSV "slaves"). In 12:10 and 14, he stresses that they must "serve" (*ʿbd*, from the same Hebrew word family as *ʿăbādîm*) Lord alone. How ironic that they now describe themselves as *Samuel's* "servants" or slaves (*ʿăbādîm* again, 12:19). While the phrase "your servants" often occurs in polite usage, here it forms part of a consistent pattern that identifies or confuses service to Samuel with service to Lord.

Samuel promises to pray/intercede for the people (12:23), adding that he will instruct them in the good and right way. Israel may have a king now, but Samuel positions himself as the arbiter of what both people and king shall do. This is not a farewell speech after all. Samuel has no intention of relinquishing his position as speaker for God.

PROPHET AND KING: ROUND 1 (1 SAMUEL 13:1–15A)

No sooner has Samuel finished his own "farewell address" than he announces God's withdrawal of support from Saul's house (the working out of which takes up most of the rest of 1 Samuel). We have already spent considerable time on 1 Samuel 13, in which Saul, although having waited "the time appointed by Samuel," is nonetheless accused of not keeping "the commandment of the Lord your God, which he commanded you" (13:8 and 13). This appears to be a reference back to Samuel's instruction to Saul in 10:8, "you shall go down to Gilgal ahead of me. . . . Seven days you shall wait, until I come to you and show you what you shall do." As presented in that verse, however, it is an instruction from Samuel, not Lord. That Samuel here presents it as Lord's command continues the pattern of his positioning of himself so close to Lord that the people cannot distinguish between Lord's command and Samuel's.

THE MISSING PROPHET (1 SAMUEL 13:15B–14:52)

In 1 Samuel 13, Samuel is present for only six verses (10–15). He arrives after Saul's troops have begun to desert and departs again before the battle, leaving Saul and six hundred men to deal with thirty thousand Philistine chariots, six thousand horsemen, and "troops like the sand on the seashore in multitude" (13:15 and 5). As far as we know, the only information Samuel gives Saul during the visit is, "Your kingdom will not continue" (13:14). We could, of course, imagine that Samuel provides wise counsel during an interval that the narrator does not describe. If advising the new king is indeed a primary role for Samuel (Jobling 1998, 120), then it is odd that Samuel is not shown acting as adviser.

I am more inclined to imagine that Samuel withholds instruction, because that fits so well with what follows in 1 Samuel 14. There Jonathan (with some success) and Saul and his priest (with less success) try to find the right balance between appropriate human initiative and reliance on Lord for guidance. While Saul is not our primary focus in this book, we should note that never, in 1 Samuel 14 or elsewhere, is Saul accused of turning to other gods. Why then does Lord reject him?

David Gunn argues that the fundamental issue is not Saul's behavior (or faithfulness) at all, but LORD's resentment over kingship (1980).

Fokkelman's interpretive line is at first glance more traditional, focusing on Saul's frequent but erratic appeal to the divine (sacrifice, oaths, starting inquiries with the priest and sometimes finishing them, sometimes not) and claiming that Saul's insecure piety "is *the* problem of the day" (1986, 60, Fokkelman's italics). Saul does not start out insecure, however. His erratic behavior follows his abandonment by Samuel, who has so forcefully declared, in 1 Samuel 12–13, the necessity of obeying LORD's commands, his own role as interpreter of those commands, and the severe punishment for Saul's honest error in judgment about a command. Fokkelman suggests that the impact of this abandonment on Saul can be seen in the ways that Saul's mistreatment of Jonathan in 1 Samuel 14 replicates Samuel's mistreatment of Saul in 1 Samuel 13 (1986, 77).

Strikingly, however, at the end of the story we receive a glowingly positive assessment of Saul's reign (14:47–51). We hear that Saul "fought against all his enemies on every side . . . wherever he turned he routed them. He . . . rescued Israel out of the hands of those who plundered them." This has much the same sound as the summary of Samuel's administration at the end of 1 Samuel 7 (although without the mention of "peace"), and it is resoundingly affirmative in its presentation of Saul. Fokkelman says that the frame created for 1 Samuel 13–14 by 13:1 and 14:47–52 creates "a strong relativization, we might almost say an undermining, of the negative image [of Saul] that the complex 13:2–14:46 leaves with the reader. . . . Thus the narrator or the redactor . . . makes it a priori impossible for the reader to remain locked in the naive position of a condemnatory attitude to Saul" (82). It is perhaps too much to say that the narrator makes it impossible to side completely with Samuel, especially considering the pro-prophet prejudices most readers bring to the book. And yet even readers strongly schooled to believe that the prophet must be right usually at least *ask* whether Samuel's treatment of Saul is fair. Intentionally or unintentionally, the mix of sources in these chapters prompts uneasiness with Samuel's role. Jobling correctly observes that "1 Samuel 14:47–52 demonstrates Saul's ability, after all, to grasp kingship—at least in the absence of Samuel" (1998, 88).

In discussing the concluding summary of Samuel's judgeship (7:13–17), I noted the dissonance between the summary's announcement of peace and subsequent reports of ongoing military trouble for Israel, not to mention the dissonance between the expectation that Samuel's death would be announced and the fact that his leadership continues for chapters beyond its "concluding summary." Similar dissonance occurs at the end of 1 Samuel 14. Verse 14:52 warns us that Saul's rescue of Israel (14:48) does not mean an end to "hard fighting," and we will soon learn that we have not by any means reached the end of Saul's story.

PROPHET AND KING: ROUND 2 (1 SAMUEL 15)

If Samuel seemed oddly absent as adviser in 1 Samuel 13–14, he is forcefully present in 1 Samuel 15. The chapter begins with Samuel instructing Saul in full-blown "thus says the LORD" messenger format. As I stated earlier, I believe that in the Samuel narratives such pronouncements can be taken as reliable quotations of LORD's word. That is, in every case where the this format is used, other information in the narrative affirms or at least does not raise doubts that LORD actually said this in the narrative world. (Whether a real-life God historically said exactly these words is a separate question about which people hold firm and varied opinions.) LORD tells Saul to "utterly destroy" (*ḥrm*) all Amalekites and their livestock.

The narrator reports that Saul does not "utterly destroy" the Amalekite king or the best of the livestock (15:8–9). However, the term "utterly destroy" is not as clear as the English translation might suggest. It involves the suspension of normal booty-taking practices during "holy war,"[17] but exact procedures are not spelled out. David Gunn argues that in Saul's understanding, a later sacrifice of the livestock at Gilgal (which is what Saul says he intends; 15:21) will fulfill the command (1980, 45–54). This would explain why Saul seems not to realize, in 15:13, 15, and 20–21, that he has disobeyed. Gunn also points out that it would be stupid to bring illicitly captured livestock to Gilgal, a major worship center, but quite logical to go there for sacrifices that one thought would fulfill a divine command. On the other hand, the shift from the narrator's statement that "*Saul and the people* spared Agag . . . and all that was valuable" to Saul's statement that "*the people* spared the best" (15:9 and 15, italics added; see also 1 S 21) does look suspicious, as if Saul senses something wrong and is shifting blame.

Unlike 1 Samuel 13, where we had only Samuel's word to go on with regard to LORD's opinion of the situation, in 1 Samuel 15:11, we hear LORD's evaluation in the form of direct quotation: "I regret that I made Saul king, for he has turned back from following me, and has not carried out my commands." Miscall points out, correctly, that this statement is not expressly tied to the particular situation with the Amalekites (1986, 102), and Brueggemann notes that LORD speaks of Saul failing to carry out "commands" (plural), not just a single command (1990, 111). However, I think that the construction of the chapter justifies the usual understanding that LORD's reaction is precipitated by Saul's handling of the Amalekite affair.[18]

At any rate, 15:11 tells us that Samuel is angry at LORD's announcement. Why? This is, for me, the most puzzling moment in Samuel's story. Traditional interpretation has generally held that Samuel wholly aligns himself with LORD's purposes, which Saul has (in this interpretation) consistently and flagrantly violated. But if so, Samuel has no reason to get upset with LORD. Tsumura suggests, with a reference to Abraham Joshua Heschel's description of the prophet as one who shares the divine *pathos*, that Samuel shares Lord's anger *at Saul* (Tsumura 2007, 396; Heschel 1962, 26). But it is not clear to me that a Samuel who shared Lord's anger at Saul would "cry out" (*zʿq*, a verb that implies distress or petitioning or both) to Lord about the matter all night.

Recent literary commentators tend to see more of a rift between God and Samuel, whose self-interest in opposing kingship they typically stress. But if, as they argue, Samuel shows an unseemly eagerness to find Saul at fault in 1 Samuel 13, why does he object to Lord's fault finding in 1 Samuel 15? In trying to answer, these interpreters continue to pursue the theme of Samuel's self-interest. "If Samuel is antagonistic toward Saul because Saul represents a challenge," says Peter Miscall, "then Samuel is angry with the Lord because his change of mind can further undermine Samuel's own position with the people. Samuel has recently proclaimed Saul king, and what will the people think if he now 'dethrones' him? Samuel prays for the lord [*sic*] to retain Saul or to maintain, in some other way, Samuel's credibility" (1986, 103; although Miscall also offers an alternative reading in which Samuel is sympathetic to Saul). We know, after all, that people do tend to hold Samuel accountable for Lord's decisions: recall how they referred to Lord as "your God" in 12:19. (Saul uses the same expression in 15:15, 21, and 30.)

Polzin goes a different direction in explaining Samuel's grieving, but retains the focus on self-interest. "God had rejected someone whom Samuel had so successfully molded to his own power-driven specifications" (1989, 154). Jobling agrees with Polzin that Samuel has held Saul to a model in which the king is to "do nothing without the permission of another," in line with the "wait until I come to you" of 10:8 rather than the "do whatever you see fit" of 10:7 (1998, 85). Jobling sees Saul's responses in 15:25 and 30 as evidence that the king "craves Samuel's continued support." Samuel himself, then, grieves the loss of "a king he can control, a king who is less than a king" (87).

This seems at least possible. Samuel knows that Lord has spotted "a man after his own heart" (13:14, a matter referred to again in 15:28). Samuel and Saul do not at this point know who that man is, although almost all readers do. (I do not believe that the narrative was aimed, at any stage of its composition, toward an audience ignorant of the direction in which it was headed.) What Samuel probably does guess (in the imaginative world of the story) is that a man after Lord's own heart will not depend on the prophet for guidance, nor will Lord any longer look to Samuel—if Lord ever has—as a friend with whom Lord can commiserate about the people's inconstancy (the "lonely at the top" interpretation of Lord's responses in 8:7–8). Under Saul, Samuel has remained important, someone who can call king and people to war with a "thus says the Lord." Under David, the story's audience knows, Samuel will drop almost out of sight. Surely Samuel himself can smell this in the wind.

However, the parallel between 3:15 (where "Samuel lay there until morning" and "was afraid to tell" Eli of LORD's sentence against Eli's family) and 15:10–11 suggests a somewhat more sympathetic interpretation of Samuel's unhappiness. The situations are not exactly the same, of course. There Samuel was young. Here he is old. There he did not know who was calling to him. Here LORD seems to communicate easily. There Samuel was "afraid"; here he is "angry." There the message concerned someone older; here it concerns someone younger. But in both cases, word of a divine rejection causes Samuel a sleepless night. Is it too much to wonder if these nighttime encounters are in some way a paired set, bookends for Samuel's prophetic career?

If affection and concern for Eli, and not simple fear of reprisal, keep Samuel awake in 1 Samuel 3, perhaps some genuine affection for Saul, identification with him, or both account for his discomfort with LORD's announcement in 15:11. I am not, of course, the first person to propose this. William Hertzberg, among others, supposes such affection between Samuel and Saul, saying that Saul is "loved . . . even by his opponent Samuel" (1964, 133). LORD has been responsible (or such would have been the young Samuel's likely interpretation) for Samuel having to leave his family at a very young age. Samuel knows that LORD elected and then cast off Eli's family. Samuel himself, once the divinely supported leader of a victorious Israel (1 S 7), has had the experience of being told that his era (and that of his sons) is past. He has already been forced to tell Saul that his kingship "will not continue" (13:14; probably meaning that Saul's son will not succeed him, with Saul's own oaths in the next chapter unwittingly confirming the doom on Jonathan). But since then Saul has accomplished mighty victories; his reign has seemed successful (14:47–48 and even 15:4–8). Saul has never, so far as we know, committed the sins of "taking" from the people that Samuel warned against in 1 Samuel 8, and his sons (unlike Eli's and Samuel's) are not corrupt. Could it be that Samuel feels genuinely sorry for Saul and is fed up with LORD's honor obsession and lack of interest in the people's well-being?

This is a delicate question to raise. A natural response might be, "But God requires obedience because God loves us and knows more than we do about our well-being." That claim is certainly prominent elsewhere in the Bible and subsequent religious traditions. But the Samuel storytellers do not seem to share that view of God. Recall that Eli's sons are remiss in their service to both LORD and the people, but LORD's indictments mention only their misbehavior toward LORD. All the interpretations of Saul's sin in 1 Samuel 13 involve some kind of insult or disobedience to LORD rather than abuse of the people. In 1 Samuel 15, LORD sends Saul and his army to war because of a generations-old grudge against the Amalekites, not because of any harm the Amalekites (much less their infants) are presently doing to Israel, and Saul's sin has been the ritual one of disposing of loot improperly.

In all this I see much to suggest that Lord (as depicted in the Samuel stories) is interested in obedience for the sake of obedience and little to suggest that Lord's primary interest is the well-being of the people. However much other parts of the Bible may represent God's stress on obedience as a path toward justice and righteousness for the people, here it appears to be an issue of divine personal pride. The book of Samuel assigns to God the sensitivities of an ancient warlord: deep concern with the loyalty of subordinates, hunger for obedience and honor, and not much concern with fairness, careful listening, or the impact of policies on the common person. I think Samuel—the focus of our concern in this chapter—has tired of being the front man for such a deity.

Of course a Samuel who feels sorry for Saul and who has lost patience with God's rejections and his own role in announcing them might also desire to have Saul kept on in order to preserve Samuel's own influence over Saul and/or the people. These explanations are not mutually exclusive. Samuel may well feel a little of both.

If Samuel does not want Saul cast off, however, why is he so harsh when he confronts Saul? I think we may see here the frustration of a middleman required to enforce a decree he does not approve of. One might hope that such a person would be gentle in administering policies that he or she considers problematic. Instead, too often, frustration that cannot be expressed against superiors is vented on inferiors. Samuel knows how easily offended Lord is and how implacable God's rejections can be. In turn Samuel replicates that implacability (as Saul replicated Samuel's in 1 Samuel 13–14), hammering at Saul about Lord's desire for obedience (15:22–23) and the finality of Saul's rejection (15:26 and 28–29).

This understanding of Samuel's feelings makes sense, I think, of his 15:29 statement that "the Glory of Israel will not recant or change his mind [*nḥm*]." That Lord does not recant (*nḥm*) is, as a general theological statement, untrue. Samuel knows it, because he heard Lord say in 15:11, "I regret [*nḥm*, same Hebrew word as 15:29] that I made Saul king." (In 15:35 the narrator confirms, "Lord was sorry [*nḥm*] that he had made Saul king.") But Samuel is not making a general theological statement. I think that he, exhausted from a night of fruitless crying out, articulates his frustrated perception of Lord's stance *in this case*. It is too bad that his words are so often and so coldly quoted as the eternal truth about God's ways.

Samuel's frustration may also express itself in his execution of the captured Amalekite king, Agag (1 S 15:32–33). I interpret this scene rather differently than Robert Polzin does. Polzin locates it in the context of a larger Deuteronomistic reflection on repentance (1989, 142–47). Saul, he observes, repents in 15:24–25, and then asks Samuel to *šwb*, "return" (NRSV) or "repent" (another meaning of the word, invoked here by Polzin), with him. Samuel refuses, and in the course of his refusal makes his theologically erroneous statement about the Glory of Israel being someone who will not repent (*nḥm*, with a meaning overlapping that of *šwb*). Saul does not let the matter rest, but again states that he has sinned and again asks Samuel to *šwb* ("repent," in Polzin's translation) with him. This time Samuel agrees (1 S 15:30–31). As Polzin understands it, Samuel has now come to share Saul's hope that Lord will respond to their repentance, a repentance symbolized by the killing of Agag. But the divine change of heart does not come. For Polzin, this is about "the salvaging of God's freedom in the light of human freedom" (142).

I am dubious about Polzin's conclusion that both Samuel and Saul hope for a divine reversal. He fails to note that in 15:31 only Saul, not Samuel, worships. I believe that Samuel, like Eli before him, has lost confidence in his intercessory power. He helps Saul save face, but he does not expect a reversal of the divine condemnation. His hewing of Agag expresses, I think, just how frustrated and helpless he feels. At some subliminal level, although probably not consciously, he may even feel that the one who deserves hewing is Lord.

I have always wondered whether Samuel's discouragement at this point becomes a self-fulfilling prophecy. What if Samuel responded to Saul's request with the "perhaps" (*ʿûlay*, also translated "it may be") used by the Philistine diviners, Saul's servant, Jonathan, and David (1 S 6:5, 9:6, 14:6, and 2 S 16:12)? Lord seems to react positively in those other cases. What if Samuel answered here, "Yes, I will worship with you, perhaps Lord will change his mind"?[19]

He does not, however. The chapter ends with images of dismemberment and separation. Agag is hewed to pieces.[20] Samuel and Saul depart to their respective hometowns, a separation narratively overemphasized by statements that "Samuel did not see Saul again until the day of his death" (not true, they meet again in 1 Samuel 19:24) and that Samuel "mourned" (NRSV "grieved," but this Hebrew word is usually used for mourning death) for Saul. Samuel returns to Ramah with a heavy heart. Lord is sorry about Saul, too, but in a different way than Samuel is.

A NEW ERA BEGINS (1 SAMUEL 16:1–13)

Chapter 16 opens with a restatement of divergence between Lord's views and Samuel's: Samuel grieves/mourns Saul (16:1, same word as 15:35) while Lord has rejected him. Lord wants Samuel to anoint a son of Jesse. Samuel protests that he cannot, for "Saul . . . will kill me" (16:2). I suspect that Samuel did not anoint David at all: notice that there is no later reference to such an anointing. When the story was circulated that he had done so, there would need to be some answer to the question, "Why has this never been mentioned?" What better answer than, "It had to be done in secret, because of Saul"?

That, however, is speculative. As the story now stands, God orders Samuel to Bethlehem. What then to make of Samuel's protest that Saul will kill him? I do not think we can take Samuel's words as evidence that Saul actually has a mortal vendetta against him, or even that Samuel believes so, given the clemency Saul has thus far shown (1 S 10:27, 11:12–13, 14:45, 15:6) and his sparing of Agag. I think Samuel is stalling, hoping to evade an unwanted assignment because he still favors Saul, and also, perhaps, because he anticipates being marginalized under the new king. The latter concern might be negatively stated as a "control issue," or more generously as Samuel's anticipation of the problems that will come with a more powerful style of king. (Jobling suggests that while LORD could have a change of heart about Saul, this option is closed in David's case; 1998, 85 and 87.) It seems strained, however, to suppose that Samuel still opposes kingship in general, for his enthusiasm rises quickly when he sees Eliab.

An earlier chapter discussed LORD's words to Samuel in this story. LORD seems to hint that the problems with Saul were Samuel's fault, although foregoing chapters have clearly indicated that LORD, not Samuel, chose Saul. Samuel, despite his reluctance and his initial enthusiasm for Eliab, does anoint LORD's chosen candidate, David. But it is a sad scene for the old prophet. He is scolded by God, and once David has arrived, we do not hear Samuel speak. Samuel goes home at the end of the story. LORD's spirit (never said to be upon Samuel, although we have seen it come upon Saul) is now "mightily upon David."

THE FADING OF SAMUEL (1 SAMUEL 19:18–24 AND 25:1)

Once David is on the scene, Samuel nearly disappears. We do not hear him instructing David (the only utterance to David by a prophet in 1 Samuel is Gad's matter-of-fact military advice in 22:5), although he does interact with David for a few verses at the end of 1 Samuel 19. Persecuted by Saul, David flees to Samuel and, we hear, settles briefly with him in Ramah. When Saul sends messengers and eventually comes himself to capture David, prophetic frenzy ensues: "He [Saul] too stripped off his clothes, and he too fell into a frenzy before Samuel. He lay naked all that day and all that night. Therefore it is said, 'Is Saul also among the prophets?'" (19:24).

Jobling attempts to read this scene through the lens of a "tutelage" model for Samuel's relationships with Saul and David. "Samuel's *new* pupil, David, looks to him for help. Samuel's rejected pupil, Saul, on seeing Samuel again, cannot avoid falling back into the old pattern of apprentice. The technique of recalling the beginning of Saul's career when he first joined Samuel's prophetic band (1 S 10:9–13) compellingly supports this reading" (1998, 121, Jobling's italics).

Jobling is undoubtedly correct that the scene recalls the beginning of Saul's career, but I question the tutelage model. I have already commented on the shortage of evidence that Samuel provides helpful instruction to Saul. Depictions of Samuel instructing David are even more conspicuous by their absence. Even in the anointing scene Samuel is not shown saying anything to David. We can imagine that David's sojourn with Samuel at Naioth must have involved some conversation, but the narrator says nothing about it, not even offering a general statement such as "Samuel taught him."

As I read it, David's coming ends Samuel's era. Samuel's speaking is no longer important. The Naioth story focuses on Saul's discomfiture, not Samuel's authority. Samuel's silent presiding shows just how diminished a role is now played by the man none of whose words God let fall to the ground. It is an odd and unsettling image for Samuel's last live appearance.

A few chapters later, in 1 Samuel 25:1, Samuel's death is announced. "All Israel" assembles and mourns for him, a last affirmation of his national importance. The one odd note is the notice that "they buried him at his home [or house] in Ramah." As Tsumura notes, "burial in one's house was unusual in Israel" (2007, 575). Both biblical and archeological evidence indicate that most burials took place in caves that could accommodate multiple members of a family (see Gen 29:49). Tsumura also notes, however, that neighboring cultures did bury their dead in their houses, partly to facilitate ongoing consultation of the ancestors (575), and it appears that veneration and consultation of ancestors took place in Israel itself (Lewis 1989).[21] While Tsumura says, "it is very unlikely that the people worshipped the dead Samuel" (575), is it coincidence that this prophet buried "at his home" will shortly appear in the Bible's only detailed story of consultation with a ghost?

ENCORE (1 SAMUEL 28:3–25)

After his death (reported again in 1 Samuel 28:3, probably because the coming story requires us to know that he is really dead), Samuel makes a final appearance. The Philistines are once again gathering for war against the Israelites. David, estranged from Saul's court, has affiliated himself with the Philistines. Saul has mustered the Israelite forces at Gilboa, but he is frightened. Once again he seeks advice from LORD, and once again LORD will not answer: "not by dreams, or by Urim [sacred lots], or by prophets" (28:6). Desperate, Saul consults a medium. He must go in disguise because he himself has already "expelled the mediums and the wizards from the land" (28:3).

To those who have grown up hearing that "a man or a woman who is a medium or a wizard shall be put to death" (Lev 20:27, see also Lev 19:31 and 20:6), Saul's action may seem self-evidently wicked. However, consultation with the ancestors, which is the process that such specialists seem to have facilitated, was a widespread Israelite practice, and it did not necessarily involve appeal to other gods. (Jobling points out that in 1 Samuel 28:10–11 the medium is perfectly happy to accept Saul's oath by LORD. "This woman is no enemy to the religion of YHWH"; 1998, 189.) Such consultation was, to be sure, opposed by the compilers of Torah's priestly and Deuteronomic law codes. The question is, why? Did LORD indeed declare to them (or Moses) that witches must die? Or did the priests and prophets of Jerusalem suppose that LORD would declare that, because they identified LORD's interests with their own power and wanted to stamp out more locally based spiritual practitioners? This is not a baseless question: Deuteronomy and the Deuteronomistic History testify to an effort to close down local places of worship in favor of the Jerusalem temple as the sole authorized site for sacrifice. (See especially 2 Kings 23:15–25, and notice that putting away mediums and wizards is part of this reform.)

For the purposes of understanding Samuel, we do not need to approve of Saul's consultation. Indeed, whatever our opinion of ancestor consultation, the very fact that Saul does something he himself has banned (according to the chapter) puts a shadow over his action. (His problematic oracle seeking and fasting link 1 Samuel 28 with 1 Samuel 14; here the curses of that earlier chapter come to rest.) However, our eagerness to condemn the "witch" (a word not used in standard translations of this chapter, although the story is often referred to as "The Witch of Endor") may blind us to the way in which the narrative actually portrays her. Her human kindness toward a man on the brink of death stands in sharp contrast to LORD's abandonment and Samuel's bitterness.

She is not a fraud. The narrator very straightforwardly calls the ghost she summons "Samuel" (28:15), indicating to me that we are not to understand the appearance as a deception. According to the storyteller, the medium can do what she promises: Samuel indeed rises and speaks to Saul. The ghost's message is at least as uncompromising as, and in content very similar to, the one delivered in 1 Samuel 15. "Because you did not obey the voice of the LORD, and did not carry out his fierce wrath against Amalek . . . the LORD will give Israel along with you into the hands of the Philistines; and tomorrow you and your sons shall be with me" (28:18–19).

Samuel's ghost does not use a messenger formula ("thus says the LORD"), but we have no reason to suspect the accuracy of his report on LORD's attitude and intentions. It is painfully consistent with other messages Samuel has delivered. "You and your sons" (28:19) reminds us of 1 Samuel 3, where Samuel had to report the condemnation of Eli and his sons. "Just as he spoke by me" (28:17) recalls the motif of identity between Samuel's word and God's. References to divine wrath in the face of disobedience continue 1 Samuel's portrayal of LORD as a deity absolutely intolerant of any disrespect. The Lord Samuel has served is a violent and demanding one, and Samuel has been the herald of that violence throughout his career.

Something we should not miss about this chapter, however, is that *Samuel speaks*. He may not have much to say that is new, but this is the first time he has spoken since David's arrival. Not only does Samuel speak, but *he speaks when Lord does not*. Lord refuses to answer Saul. Samuel's ghost does answer, however harshly. Here in Samuel's curtain call, as in so many previous stories, there seems a slight dissonance between Samuel and the Lord he serves. Could Lord's plans for Saul be as bitter for Samuel's ghost to pronounce as they are for Saul to hear?

CHAPTER 6

SAMUEL, HIS GOD, AND US

The story of Samuel unsettles many common assumptions about the Bible, its prophets, and its God. In the first chapter, I mentioned a youth minister who chose 1 Samuel 3 as the sermon text for his ordination. He wanted to make the point that God has purposes even for children. He trimmed the reading to omit what God actually says to Samuel. For this young minister, as for most modern Bible readers, the portrayal of God in the Samuel stories was highly discomfiting. The historical accuracy of the stories was not an article of faith for him, and he was comfortable with the general idea of divergence between biblical worldviews and our own. But he believed in the God of Axial and post-Axial monotheism, a God with strong ethical standards but also extraordinary forbearance and steadfast love. He recognized the tension between that view and the presentation of LORD in the scripture he had chosen.

The students who questioned the fairness of Samuel's denunciation of Saul in 1 Samuel 13 experienced a similar disconnect between the story and their presuppositions. They expected God's prophet to present a principled message, not a barrage of accusations that ignored Saul's reported obedience, the urgency of the situation, and Samuel's own failure to arrive as promised. The conflict between their expectations and what they read was so uncomfortable that they sought resolution by discounting what they had noticed about Samuel's arbitrariness.

Samuel's story also challenges our expectation that the Bible, or at least any given biblical book, will present a unified message. Most first-time (or even many-time) readers of 1 Samuel do not notice conflicting reports on such issues as whether there was peace all Samuel's days or whether Samuel saw Saul again after the hewing of Agag. Some do notice tension between the positive presentation of kingship in 1 Samuel 9–11 and claims in 1 Samuel 8 and 12 that to ask for a king is to reject LORD. Once we notice them, such conflicts and tensions demand explanation.

Source and redaction critics point to such discontinuities as evidence of a complex history of composition. I find their speculations believable and helpful. Others reject the particular compositional theories I have presented or even the whole idea of the story's development over time, but it seems to me that even at the level of interpreting the present text, the model of a story told by several tellers works better than straining to explain away discontinuities. To me, multivoicedness is not simply a compositional hypothesis but a literary feature of the present book of 1 Samuel.

What is the impact of this multivoicedness, once we recognize it? The transitions between voices disturb our immersion in the imagined world of the story, making us aware of the tellers who stand between us and Samuel. We may not know exactly who they are, but their telling reveals something about their attitudes and agendas. The most prominent voices emphasize prophetic authority, especially with regard to LORD's legitimation or rejection of other leaders. Others would prefer that prophets do the leading themselves. Some seem optimistic about the possibilities of life in the world under LORD, others seem to regard Israel's history as a plunge toward inevitable disaster. The jostling between their viewpoints frustrates our desire to be presented with a single right solution to the questions under discussion.

SAMUEL

The book of 1 Samuel remembers Samuel himself as a figure of immense power, someone similar to Moses and Joshua (see also Ps 99:6). He is not only prophet but judge and perhaps priest as well, performing functions associated with all three of these kinds of leaders. LORD lets none of his words fall to the ground (1 S 3:19). Samuel can dismiss priests and kings or anoint them. When he summons "all Israel," all Israel responds—repeatedly. When he cries out to LORD, LORD thunders in response (7:9–10, 12:18). When Israel completely heeds Samuel's word, the Philistines withdraw and return the towns they have captured, at least according to 1 Samuel 7.

Yet Samuel does have human weaknesses. He grows old, and although his sons do not follow in his ways, he places them in power (8:1–5). He will not then admit that there is a problem; instead he responds peevishly to the people's request for new leadership (8:6, 12:1–3). There is some question about how carefully he differentiates between his own commandments and evaluations and LORD's (13:13, 16:6). Unlike Moses and Joshua, who remain in good health and full power until they die with their farewell orations still ringing in our ears, Samuel declines gradually from victorious judge to scolding prophet to unsuccessful intercessor to silent anointer of David and presider over Saul's frenzy, hauled up from his grave at the end by an illicit female medium.

People remember Samuel's human weaknesses, however, less than they remember the denunciations he delivers on LORD's behalf. Samuel does occasionally serve as LORD's agent for acts of salvation and establishment: the victories of 1 Samuel 7, the designation and installation of Saul in 1 Samuel 9–10, and the anointing of David in 1 Samuel 16. These acts of establishment, however, do not seem to "stick." There is not peace "all the days of Samuel," Saul has to be deposed, and even David turns out to be problematic, at least from the people's point of view (Steussy 1999,

49–96). More potent are Samuel's acts of disestablishment, from the announcement of disinheritance for Eli in 1 Samuel 3 through the condemnations of Saul to the prediction of Saul's death in 1 Samuel 28, not to mention the threat that "in that day" Israel will cry out because of the king it has chosen and will receive no answer (8:18). The emphasis on disestablishment may be directly traceable to the character of the Lord Samuel serves, for that Lord is presented in the Samuel stories as more adept at destruction than construction.

The picture of Samuel as Lord's agent and conduit is complicated by the dissonance between Lord and Samuel. We see it first when Samuel is "afraid to tell the vision to Eli" (1 S 3:15). It comes up again in Samuel's only-partly-reported conversation with Lord about the people's request for a king (8:6–9). The narrator does not tell us exactly what displeases Samuel, but we gather from Lord's reply that Lord and Samuel do not see eye to eye. Samuel may be distancing himself from Lord's decision about a king in 10:17–24, where he proclaims the king is Lord's choice, without adding his own endorsement. The narrator openly states that Samuel is angry after Lord's announcement in 15:11, although we do not know the exact nature of Samuel's complaint. Samuel's feelings about Saul remain different from Lord's in 1 Samuel 15:35 and 16:1. This disagreement sets up a tension that continues through the anointing of David in 16:1–13 and perhaps finds a final echo in 1 Samuel 28, where Samuel's ghost speaks to Saul when Lord refuses to do so.

If the storytellers want us to see the prophet as reliable proclaimer of Lord's word, why do they show us these tensions between the prophet and Lord? When I put that question to Antony Campbell, he suggested in an e-mail (June 22, 2009) that casting the story in this way defuses accusations that the prophets are pursuing personal agendas. We can imagine someone saying, "How do we know that Lord rejected Saul? You know Samuel never liked Saul. Maybe it was just Samuel's idea." The storyteller might answer, "Oh, no, that could not have been it, because Samuel was terribly upset, in fact he cried out to Lord all night!"

Campbell's answer makes sense, and it might apply to a whole series of stories and oracles in which a prophet protests Lord's decision (see for instance Amos 7:1–9, just preceding Amos's denial that he is a prophet). An additional effect of the technique, which would also work to the advantage of prophetic storytellers, is that it shifts the blame for what may be unpopular decisions from prophet to Lord: "Look, don't get angry at Samuel for denouncing Saul. Samuel didn't want to do it, he only did it because Lord made him."

Whatever the original rhetorical purpose of the motif, it has caused me to feel sorry for Samuel. However harsh I think he is in 1 Samuel 15, I can understand how hard it might have been for him to announce a decision with which he disagrees.

The Lord to whom his mother dedicates him before conception is a harsh master, and Samuel's job is one I do not envy, however beguiling the thought of praying for thunder and getting it. I think better of Samuel because of the night he spends crying out for Saul, even if I also think that a less curmudgeonly, more helpful Samuel, a Samuel who stuck around and gave Saul some advice after crowning him, might have been able to help Saul stay out of trouble to begin with. (Then again, given Lord's surly attitude toward kingship, perhaps Saul never had a chance.)

Samuel's service to Lord divides him from his birth family, his adoptive family, and the first king of Israel. Samuel never seems to establish a standing relationship with the second king, David. Were his sons not mentioned (1 S 8:1–5 and 12:2), we would never suspect that Samuel was married or had children. It seems unlikely that he felt proud of his sons, given their performance. As compensation for all these broken or never-established human relationships, Lord might have served as friend or father to Samuel, but never (with the possible exception of 1 Samuel 8:7–8, and I think not even there) do we see Lord offer Samuel comfort. The medium calls up Samuel's ghost in 1 Samuel 28 because Lord refuses to speak to Saul. So far as we know, since 16:12 Lord has not spoken to Samuel, either.

The feisty Spanish saint Teresa of Avila reportedly once said to God, "If this is the way you treat your friends, it's no wonder you have so few" (Barry 2008, 127). I can imagine Samuel making the same comment. That takes us, however, from Samuel to Samuel's God.

GOD

Samuel's Lord is fixated on issues of obedience and wields power not bound by even his own promises (see 1 S 2:30 and 2 S 7:15). In part this is because the writers deduce Lord's character from the events of a militarily insecure, agriculturally unstable, and medically unexplained world. In part it is because the stories come to us from a social world dominated by the categories of honor and shame—recall Hannah's distress over Peninnah's humiliating taunts. When the writers portray Lord as angry at the disrespectful behavior of Eli's sons or unable to forget wrongs done by Amalek generations earlier, they describe a God who shares their own cultural sensibilities.

Human dealings with this Lord seem driven partly by hunger for status (so, for instance, Hannah's request for a child or Saul's face-saving worship in 1 Samuel 15:30–31) but above all by fear. The Philistines fear Lord when the ark comes into the Israelite camp and later after plague breaks out in their cities. The Israelites fear the Philistines, a fear appealed to by Samuel when he orders them to put aside foreign gods (1 S 7:3). However, the Israelites also fear Lord's own anger, particularly after the loss of the ark, the smiting of the Beth-shemeshites, and the harvest-destroying thunderstorm prayed for by Samuel. Saul is often criticized for hiding among the bags when lots are cast to choose a king, but if he is afraid of how a king will fare at Lord's and Samuel's hands, his fears are justified.

In light of Lord's fearsomeness, it is not surprising that the Samuel stories touch repeatedly on the theme of intercession for offenses against Lord. Eli questions the possibility of such intercession (1 S 2:25). Samuel demonstrates that such intercession is possible and can succeed (1 S 7) and promises to continue performing it (1 S 12). He also indicates, however, that under some conditions Lord might refuse to answer (1 S 8), and in 1 Samuel 15:11 his intercession for Saul fails, after which Samuel refuses to try again.

The tellers of the Prophetic Record, I suspect, claim authority like Samuel's to endorse or repudiate leaders and to intercede with Lord on behalf of the people. They want people to know that Lord is inscrutable and dangerous because then people will understand why they need prophets and need to listen to them. The Josianic storytellers likely hoped to make the case that the people's well-being depended on their response to prophetic calls for repentance and obedience. The final Deuteronomistic redactors, writing after the monarchy had fallen, may have been especially interested in the hope that, even without kings, Lord can provide adequate leadership.

Yet however sincere their desire to promote a healthy relationship between the people and Lord, the storytellers' zeal leads them to emphasize (perhaps quite unintentionally) the worst features of the Lord they endorse. Indeed I wonder if for this reason the Samuel stories may present a religious outlook grimmer than that actually held by most people in the time the stories were written. In emphasizing Lord's fearsomeness, the tellers risk distancing the people from Lord. Allow me to contrast an incident from Samuel's story with another scriptural tale of prophetic intercession. In this second story, a prophet and Lord spar over responsibility for a people that has just erected a golden calf at the foot of the mountain: "The Lord said to Moses, 'Go down at once! *Your* people, whom *you* brought up out of the land of Egypt, have acted perversely.' . . . But Moses implored the Lord his God, and said, 'O Lord, why does your wrath burn hot against *your* people whom *you* brought out of the land of Egypt?'" (Ex 32:7 and 11, italics added). In 1 Samuel, by contrast, prophet and people spar over responsibility for the *God* that they must deal with: "Samuel said to the people, . . . 'If both you and the king who reigns over you will follow the Lord *your* God, it will be well.' . . . All the people said to Samuel, 'Pray to the Lord *your* God for your servants, so that we may not die'" (1 S 12:6, 14, and 19, italics added).

When a prophet calls down thunderstorms or a pastor claims power to bring pink slips, the intent may be to bring people into alignment with Lord's wishes—as interpreted, of course, by the leader in question. The actual effect, however, may be that people come to think of that God as "yours" rather than "ours."

US

Permeating the story of Samuel is a vision that if LORD's people would just listen to their leaders, and the leaders would just listen to LORD, then LORD would fend off threatening enemies, bringing peace and well-being to the people. As different voices enter the telling, they give us variations on this theme. Some believe that in such a world a king would handle the people's military affairs, although such a king would have to be obedient to LORD's commands as delivered by LORD's prophets. Others envision religious, military, and civil leadership united in the one figure of a prophet like Moses or Samuel. In this variation LORD would raise up subsequent leaders as required and the people would never be beholden to a single royal dynasty. Although the stories recognize that a prophet can have human foibles and even object on occasion to the tasks assigned by LORD, they seem confident about the possibility of having leaders through whom LORD's word comes reliably.

Stories elsewhere in the canon acknowledge that even in ancient Israel the question of who speaks for LORD was not so easily answered. Micaiah faces off against the four hundred (other) prophets of the king of Israel (1 K 22), Amos against Amaziah (Amos 7), and Jeremiah against Hananiah (Jer 28). With all the clarity of hindsight, biblical narrators designate some of these as true speakers for LORD and some as liars. For people standing there at the time, the decisions would have been less clear.

However difficult it might be to distinguish true prophets from false, we might manage if prophets really fell into such distinct categories. But even the truest contemporary prophets have limitations, blindnesses, and outright flaws. Inspired word comes mixed with human agendas (as I suspect it always has). Prophets' opponents may also possess pieces of the truth (and pieces of falsehood). I have treated "thus says the LORD" statements in the Samuel stories as narratively (although perhaps not historically or even theologically) reliable quotations of LORD's word. In real life "thus says the LORD" comes with no such guarantee. Elders may discern that even the most respected, admired, and perhaps feared pastor is no longer making the decisions that best advance God's work.

We can respect and even share the longing of the Samuel writers for a world in which simple obedience would solve everything, but those writers cannot tell us whose "thus says the LORD"—if anyone's—we should honor today. They do not even offer us a set of values on which to make such judgments (although elsewhere in the Bible we may find more guidance). They do, perhaps, show us what religion turns into when fear (of the world's dangers and of God's own power) becomes its primary motivation.[1] And they show us how easy it can be for religious leaders, in their jockeying for power, to distance people from God.

I would dearly love to be able to say that the pre-Axial God of Samuel is a museum piece, a souvenir of a religious outlook that we have left far behind. But religions seldom leave anything behind. The idea of God as a partisan warrior who will champion our cause as long as we repay the favor with obedience and flattery is still very much alive, and we would do well to consider its practical and theological consequences. I sometimes suggest to students that they treat the books of Samuel as a theological experiment. If you interpret everything that happens as a direct reflection of divine will, what kind of God will you end up with? A God who is not particularly loving or lovable and who is not a champion of the oppressed. In the face of such a God, for whom "might makes right," the obvious human response is to give up on questions of fairness or goodness and to do what God wants to avoid God's displeasure. And that plays, of course, right into the hands of those who claim to speak for such a God.

The student who reported the pink-slip drama felt sympathy for Samuel and his modern counterpart, but he was not ready to buy their claims wholesale. I share his mix of sympathy and caution. I would not want to walk in Samuel's shoes, but sympathy does not require that I submit to Samuel's view of God.

NOTES

1. INTRODUCTION

1. The Hebrew text of this and many other Bible passages refers to God by an actual proper name, spelled with the consonants YHWH and incorrectly rendered in English during the middle ages as "Jehovah." Most Christians have followed the Jewish custom of saying "the Lord" when this name is encountered, rather than pronouncing the actual name. Translators mark the situation by using large and small caps for "LORD" in places where the Hebrew text says YHWH. (English "Lord," without the small caps, translates an honorific title rather than God's proper name.) I will respect the tradition of using LORD, but in order to preserve the sense that we are really dealing with a name, rather than a title, I will (except when quoting other authors) use LORD without the definite article: "LORD" rather than "the LORD."

2. See page 105, note 9, and page 108, note 14.

3. Eslinger makes a similar observation: "When the narrator tells us that Yahweh 'did not allow his words to fall to the ground' we can only believe that Yahweh shaped the course of events to agree with the words" (1985, 156).

2. SOURCES OF THE SAMUEL STORIES

1. What we mean by "the Bible" depends on whether we are Jews, Roman Catholics, Anglicans, Protestants, or members of one of the Eastern Orthodox churches, but although these groups use different sets of biblical books, all of them face the kinds of issues I describe here.

2. The idea that Samuel, Nathan, and Gad together wrote the books of Samuel may be implied by 1 Chronicles 29:29, which speaks of "the records of the seer Samuel, and . . . the records of the prophet Nathan, and . . . the records of the seer Gad." We do not know, however, whether this is a reference to our present Samuel books, and if it is, it may still be an after-the-fact guess at their authorship.

3. For photographs and transcription of the Dead Sea Samuel scrolls, see Cross (2005). For an English translation, see Abegg, Flint, and Ulrich (1999).

4. For a manageable overview of these compositional theories, I recommend the articles "Samuel, Book of 1–2" and "Deuteronomistic History" in the *Anchor Bible Dictionary.* For a more detailed treatment, see Antony F. Campbell and Mark A. O'Brien's *Unfolding the Deuteronomistic History* (2000).

5. Campbell points to the parallels between the anointings of Saul, David, and Jehu (1 S 9–10 and 16, 2 K 9; Campbell 1986, 17–23) and the dismissals of Jeroboam, Ahab,

and Jehu. Note, for instance, the torn-cloak motif linking Jeroboam's dismissal to Saul's (1 S 15, 1 K 11:29–39; Campbell 1986, 39–45).

6. McCarter writes, "It [the prophetic history] stood alongside the Deuteronomic legislation itself among the received resources of the Deuteronomistic school, having arisen originally in circles of thought that were to some degree ancestral to the school's theology" (1980a, 22).

7. McCarter (1980a) points out several instances where the copyist of 1 Samuel seems to have made mistakes.

8. Gunn (1990) offers similar comments about Sternberg's (1985) omniscient or perhaps omnipotent narrator.

3. THE MANY ROLES OF SAMUEL

1. We find references to Samuel as prophet in 1 Chronicles 29:29 and 2 Chronicles 35:18 (as well as its parallel in 1 Esdras 1:20) and as seer in 1 Chronicles 9:22, 26:8, and 29:29. (1 Esdras appears in Eastern Orthodox Bibles but not the western Roman Catholic and Protestant canons; it was likely composed in the second century B.C.E. Parts of it are very similar to 2 Chronicles, Ezra, and Nehemiah, and it likely drew upon forms of those books earlier than or divergent from the ones that found their way into the Jewish canon. It also contains some material not found in those books. You can find the text of 1 Esdras with notes in NRSV study Bibles such as Harrelson, ed., *The New Interpreter's Study Bible: New Revised Standard Version with the Apocrypha* [2003]; Meeks and Bassler, eds., *The HarperCollins Study Bible: New Revised Standard Version with the Apocryphal/Deuterocanonical Books* [1993]; and Coogan, ed., *The New Oxford Annotated Bible with the Apocrypha, New Revised Standard Version* [2007].) Sirach (an apocryphal book also known as Ecclesiasticus or the Wisdom of Jesus Ben Sira) refers to Samuel as "a prophet of the Lord" (46:13); and in the New Testament, Acts 3:24 and 13:20 appear to include Samuel among the prophets.

2. On the struggles within the priesthood, see Hanson (1986, chapters 6–10).

3. In 1 Samuel 14:3, the phrase "priest of the LORD in Shiloh" could, in Hebrew as in English, conceivably refer to either Ahijah or Eli, but I do not think there is any doubt that the chapter depicts Ahijah as a priest.

4. According to 1 Samuel 22:20 and other verses, Abiathar is the son rather than father of Ahimelech, and Ahitub is Ahimelech's father.

5. There is a minor divergence between the Greek and Hebrew texts of 1 Samuel 1:1, but NRSV and NIV are probably correct in following the Greek text in describing Samuel's father Elkanah, toward the beginning of the verse, as "a Zuphite, from the hill country of Ephraim." This translation agrees with the end of the verse, which traces Elkanah's lineage to "Zuph, an Ephraimite." The Hebrew word at the end of the verse, *ʾeprātî*, could alternatively be translated "Ephrathite," which would make Samuel a member of David's clan; see 1 Samuel 17:12. Either way (Ephraimite or Ephrathite), he would not be a "Levite," unless (1) he was indeed a priest and (2) at this early period

"Levite" was simply another word for priest, which some have suggested was the case. First Chronicles 6:33–38 places Zuph in the tribe of Levi, but this is likely done precisely to clear up the problem of a non-Levite undertaking priestly activities (compare the modification in 1 Chronicles 18:17 of the statement in 1 Samuel 8:18 about David's sons being priests). The Chronicles genealogy contradicts the clear statement in 1 Samuel 1:1 that Zuph is an *ʾeprātî*.

6. No inquiry on David's behalf is mentioned in the account in 1 Samuel 21 of David's visit to Nob, so we do not know whether Ahimelech is telling the truth about it in 22:15, but his words to Saul confirm that such inquiry was the kind of thing a priest would be expected to do.

7. The Hebrew text of 1 Samuel 14:18 mentions the "ark," but the Greek texts, which say "ephod," are probably correct, since the ark is nowhere else connected with divination and is supposed to be in storage in Kiriath-Jearim at this point.

8. It is a bit of a surprise to find Moses designated a priest in this psalm: although Moses was from the tribe of Levi, he is usually referred to as a prophet. This is a good example of the overlap between the ideal priest and prophet, especially where Moses is concerned.

9. An interesting footnote to this story: the prophet Jeremiah, centuries down the line, is said to be a priest from Anathoth (Jer 1:1), hence presumably a descendant of Eli.

10. It also supports the suspicion that the Elide genealogy for Zadok in 2 Samuel 8:17 is wrong, since the "faithful priest" is supposed to be from a house other than Eli's.

11. A later tradition in 1 Chronicles 6:33 links a guild of levitical singers to Samuel's line, but this hardly compares to the priestly status that the Zadokites (whether or not actually descended from Zadok) eventually attain.

12. The Hebrew letter that I have transliterated *ö* is pronounced like an English *sh*, and the *p* in this word is soft, so *šōpēṭ* is pronounced *show-FAYT.*

13. The poetic version of Deborah's victory in Judges 4 names Ephraim, Benjamin, Machir (a subset of the tribe of Manasseh), Zebulun, Issachar, and Naphtali and specifically says that Reuben, Gilead (where Gad settled), Dan, and Asher did not participate in the fight. The tribes of Judah and Simeon go unmentioned.

14. For completeness I should note that not every leader in Judges is described with words from the *špṭ* family. In the last nine chapters, the terminology appears only twice (15:20 and 16:31; both occurrences refer to Samson). Of the "major judges" toward the beginning of the book, only Deborah and Jephthah are said to *špṭ* (the word is not used for Ehud or Gideon). *Špṭ* appears mostly in the general programmatic statements (2:16–19) and in summary statements for "minor deliverers" about whom no detailed stories are told. Yet under the power of the programmatic structure, we think of all the major characters of the book as "judges."

15. Killing yoked cattle in the field seems to be an ancient symbol of high emotion and determination: the Beth-shemeshites kill the cows that pulled the ark's cart (1 S

6:14), and Elisha sacrifices his plowing oxen in 1 Kings 19:21. We might also compare Saul's action to the Levite's treatment of his concubine's body in Judges 19:29–30.

16. The justice-oriented ideal of the prophet and a sense of tension between priestly and prophetic roles can be found even among those who have a more positive idea of priesthood. So, for instance, ordination committees may urge candidates to reflect on how they will combine their "priestly" (sacramental and pastoral) and "prophetic" (calling the congregation's attention to areas where they fall religiously or ethically short) roles. Here the words "priestly" and "prophetic" are used to differentiate between parts of the ordained minister's work but with the assumption that both are legitimate and needed and can be performed by the same person.

17. Such tension also appears in the layers of the Deuteronomistic History compiled after Jerusalem's fall in 586/587 B.C.E.

18. I speak of "the *reported* speech of the prophets themselves" (italics added) because we have, of course, only the narrator's word with regard to what the prophets said.

19. A list of the Bible translations I use, with their abbreviations, appears on page xi. Recall that translations in this book are from the NRSV unless I indicate otherwise.

20. For detailed discussion of true versus false prophets, see Crenshaw (1971).

21. By "inspired," I mean that it comes directly from LORD via vision or word rather than through such technical means as the ephod and lots; see Koch's discussion of inductive and intuitive divination (1982, 7–14). Ecstatic prophets are a bit of an exception: we seldom see them announcing messages, although the Bible does seem to understand them as being directly influenced by God.

22. The book printed as 2 Esdras in the NRSV study Bibles I have recommended (Harrelson 2003, Meeks and Bassler 1993, Coogan 2007) appears as 3 Esdras in the Slavonic Bible and is sometimes printed as 4 Esdras in Latin Bibles, although it is not part of the official Roman Catholic canon. The part that mentions Samuel was probably composed by a Jewish writer in the late first century C.E.

4. THE PROBLEMATIC GOD OF SAMUEL

1. I choose these textual limits for very practical reasons—this is a book about Samuel—but boundaries do influence findings. David Jobling has an excellent discussion of the consequences of our choice of boundaries, especially with respect to whether we read the canonical book of 1 Samuel or whether we follow the structural markers of the Deuteronomistic History, reading 1 Samuel 1–12 as the end of the story begun in Judges and 1 Samuel 13–31 as the beginning of a story that continues through 2 Samuel 7 (Jobling 1998, 41–125).

2. An example of conflict between a character's words and the narrator's occurs with regard to the circumstances of Israel's request for a king. According to the narrator in 1 Samuel 8, the elders request a king in response to Samuel's aging and his appointment of his corrupt sons, and the Ammonite king Nahash does not begin his oppressions until after Saul has been anointed (11:1; the Masoretic Text lacks the section on

Nahash in 10:27). But in 12:12, Samuel reverses this sequence, saying the people requested a king after Nahash's move against Israel.

3. My guess at Samuel's age is based on the likely age of weaning in that society. Information on the bull's age comes from the Greek, Syriac, and Qumran versions of 1:24 (reflected in NRSV's translation). The received Hebrew text of this verse has three bulls rather than a three-year-old bull (see the NRSV note).

4. If, on the other hand, Hannah's desire is not to raise a child but only to be free of the shame of barrenness, a shame perhaps intensified by the belief that barrenness was divinely caused (1:5–6), then the birth in itself does satisfy her wish.

5. Other biblical stories of barren women becoming the mothers of important men involve Sarai, Rebekah, and Rachel (Gen 16, 25:21, and 30), Samson's mother (Jdg 13), Elizabeth (Lk 2), and perhaps the Shunammite woman whose son is later resurrected (2 K 4; although here the most important part of the son's destiny seems to be his resurrection by Elisha). The only explicitly barren woman whose story does not eventuate in a child is Saul's daughter Michal, who is said in 2 Samuel 6:23 to have "had no child until the day of her death." This is usually interpreted as LORD's punishment of her for her criticism of David, although it might also be seen as David's punishment of her, her punishment of David, or even a divine withholding from David, and there is additionally a question about whether she might have had children prior to the scene in 2 Samuel 6 (Clines and Eskenazi 1991; Steussy 1999, 73–74 and 205n7).

6. For more on the textual variations, see McCarter (1980a, 53–55).

7. The NRSV, following a Greek textual tradition, contains another more explicit allusion to Samson in 1 Samuel 12:11. The traditional Hebrew text of that verse reads "Samuel" rather than "Samson." The textual variation confirms that parallels between Samuel and Samson were being thought about somewhere in the transmission of the tradition.

8. Elsewhere Tsumura says, "The text must be very early, even pre-Davidic, if Hannah, by the spirit of God . . . prophesied about the future before the actual institution of kingship was introduced to Israel" (2007, 150). This sentence could easily be understood as attributing the song to Hannah, although technically Tsumura says only that it would be early *if* it were from Hannah. He avoids a clear statement of his position on this issue.

9. LORD left Saul king while transferring divine support to someone else, and LORD afflicted Saul with an evil spirit that prompted attacks on David (16:14 and 23, 18:10 and 19:9; see also Gunn 1980, 116–23).

10. The traditional answer, of course, is that we place our hope in a God who is both powerful and fair. The equally traditional comeback is, "If God is so powerful and so fair, how do we explain the world's unfairness?" Assessing the many possible answers to this question is beyond the scope of this book; Crenshaw (2004) gives a good discussion of the Hebrew Bible's responses. However, the books of Samuel are a particularly difficult place to assert the fairness of God.

11. Thorkild Jacobsen's *Treasures of Darkness* (1976) offers a good discussion of how human language for God is conditioned by human experience and culture, with specific reference to Mesopotamia and the ancient Near East. His discussion of ruler and parent metaphors for the gods (chapters 3 and 5) will be of special interest to readers of the present book, although I think Jacobsen gives insufficient attention to the ways in which ancient governmental models themselves employed family metaphors, creating constant cross-fertilization between the lord/servant and parent/child metaphors. For an example of this cross-fertilization, see Moran (1963) on "love" in Deuteronomy.

12. Notice that I say, "LORD's *reported* evaluation." LORD might have thought more than is reported, but all we have to go on is what the narrator tells us.

13. A common example of such eisegesis is the frequently encountered assertion that in 2 Samuel 12 God rebukes David for abusing royal power, specifically in regard to the taking of women. But the chapter does not say that LORD opposes the taking of women. Instead LORD (according to Nathan's "thus said the LORD" speech) claims credit for having already taken women and given them to David, and LORD says more could have been had for the asking (12:8). LORD's gripe is not that women have been taken, but that David did it *without asking* ("you have despised me"; 12:9–10), and part of LORD's punishment will be the further taking of women, this time *from* David (12:11), without apparent regard for the women themselves.

14. LORD specifies that there can be no expiation "by sacrifice or offering" (1 S 3:14), which might offer a loophole. Could there be nonsacrificial expiation, and is that what allows Elide descendant Jeremiah's close relationship to LORD?

15. Some find it very important that in this verse LORD speaks not of a king but simply a "ruler" (Hebrew *nāgîd*). This term (which the Deuteronomistic History uses in 1 Samuel 9:16, 10:1, 13:14, and 25:30; 2 Samuel 5:2, 6:21, and 7:8; plus four times in the books of Kings) probably means "designated one." It seems to be used for kings who have been identified but have not yet taken office or when reminding a reigning king of his status as LORD's designated leader (Mettinger 1976, 151–84).

16. The Hebrew text provides no warrant for capitalizing the helpful spirit but leaving the evil spirit in lower case, as happens in KJV ("the Spirit of the LORD departed from Saul, and an evil spirit from the LORD troubled him") followed by ASV, RSV, NIV, NKJ, and NLT.

17. Even in the Deuteronomistic History as a whole, we find relatively little talk of LORD as someone who loves. Deuteronomy itself uses the language of love (Hebrew *ʾhb,* most often used in intimate human sexual, family, or friendship contexts) six times to describe LORD's attitude toward humans (Dt 4:37, 7:8, 7:13, 10:15, 10:18, 23:5, with the love directed toward Israel, its ancestors, and in one case "the strangers"). Deuteronomy also refers a few times (5:10, 7:9 and 12) to LORD's "steadfast love," *ḥesed,* a term referring to loyalty or favor especially in contexts involving political or extended kin obligations (often the word "covenant" is present or implied). The Deuteronomistic History proper (Josh, Jdg, 1 and 2 S, and 1 and 2 K) uses *ḥesed* terminology for LORD several

times (1 S 20:14, 2 S 2:6, 7:15, 9:3, 15:20, 22:26, 22:51, 1 K 3:6, 8:23), especially in connection with LORD's favor and faithfulness toward David and Solomon. It uses words from the *ʾhb* family ("love" in the usual English sense) to describe LORD's attitude only twice: in the narrator's statement that LORD loved Solomon (2 S 12:24) and the Queen of Sheba's exclamation, upon seeing Solomon's accomplishments and wealth, that LORD must surely love Israel (1 K 10:9).

18. For a book-length popular treatment of the Axial Age, see Armstrong (2007).

19. Carl G. Jung offers a savage but insightful analysis of what Revelation says about God in his *Answer to Job* (2002). His comments on the presentation of God in some of the older Hebrew Bible writings are consistent with my conclusions in this chapter.

20. For more on God's favoritism toward David, see Steussy (2000).

5. A SEQUENTIAL READING OF SAMUEL

1. A hermeneutic is a strategy for finding meaning. The hermeneutics of suspicion, famously attributed to the eighteenth-century philosophers Karl Marx, Friedrich Nietzsche, and Sigmund Freud in Paul Ricoeur's *Freud and Philosophy* (1970, 33), have dominated humanities scholarship in recent decades. The phrase "hermeneutics of charity" comes from oral tradition about my professor Walter Harrelson in the Graduate Department of Religion at Vanderbilt University.

2. For more on the nazirite language and allusions of 1 Samuel 1, see chapter 4.

3. There is a bit of textual uncertainty about the bull, but "three years old" seems likely.

4. As I noted in chapter 4, it seems unlikely that a historical Hannah ever said the words in 2:2–10. However, the Hannah of our imagined story world does say them.

5. Meir Sternberg (1985) does a nice job of exploring the effects created by gaps between what the narrator knows, what readers know, and what characters know in biblical narrative. I disagree, however, with his thesis that the biblical God should always be understood as omniscient (did God know Saul would disappoint him?) and that the narrative is always constructed to bring our viewpoint into alignment with God's. See also Gunn's 1990 critique.

6. There has been considerable discussion about the extent of this source and whether it would originally have included 2 Samuel 6, in which David recovers the ark from Kiriath-Jearim and brings it to Jerusalem. See Campbell (1975).

7. As I noted in chapter 4, there is no prior indication of their unfaithfulness to LORD; Eslinger (1985, 234) argues that they turn to foreign gods in response to LORD's slaughter in 1 Samuel 6:19.

8. Bailey (1995, 222) suggests that God's direct intervention is required because Samuel has failed to lead the people into battle himself, but I have difficulty seeing criticism for Samuel in this story.

9. At the end of 1 Samuel 12, Samuel claims the power to instruct Israel even after the king is in place. Could we then say that Samuel "governs" even after Saul is in

power? However tempting this solution, I think it is playing games with the meaning of 1 Samuel 7:15.

10. See Gunn (1990) for a cogent and somewhat different reflection on narratorial unreliability in the Samuel books.

11. I agree here with Jobling's observation that Samuel's death "is fully staged on two separate occasions. . . . But he lives on" (1998, 253).

12. One might object that we also had a dynastic principle with Eli (and previous priests), but the function of governance (*špṭ*) did not automatically go with priesthood, at least prior to the Second Temple period. As the Deuteronomic History presents matters, hereditary priestly service existed alongside and ordinarily separate from the non-dynastic leadership of judges and the dynastic leadership of kings.

13. Jobling (1998, 62–63) attributes Samuel's action to the fact that "the narrative is under intolerable pressure" because kingship must be understood both as God's will (because it happened) and as a violation of that will (since it turned out badly).

14. The comparable point I have in mind is the beginning of 2 Samuel 6. Hitherto there has been not a hint of divine displeasure with anything David has done, although humanly speaking some of his actions have seemed questionable. I think his move to bring the ark into his new capital, Jerusalem, bespeaks an assumption on David's part that Lord can always be counted on to support him. Uzzah's death shakes David up considerably, probably because it brings that assumption into question (Steussy 1999, 59–60).

15. As I have noted earlier, 1 Samuel 9:16 and 10:1 use the term "ruler" (*nāgîd*) for Saul rather than "king," but as the narrative is presently put together, Saul is clearly anointed for kingship.

16. These similarities have prompted many, although not all, scholars to consider 1 Samuel 12 Deuteronomistic. Even Robert Alter, who seldom speculates about sources, speaks here of "clusters of Deuteronomistic verbal formulas" (1999, 67).

17. The most famous story about *ḥrm* is probably the story of Achan in Joshua 6:16–21 and 7:1–26. Notice that after the extermination of Achan and his family, Lord issues a new set of instructions that allow the taking of booty (Josh 8:1–2). Although Saul is harshly denounced for taking Amalekite spoil, David's taking of Amalekite spoils in 1 Samuel 30—he uses part of it to curry favor with the Judean elders who will soon anoint him king—evokes no condemnation.

18. The statement by Samuel's ghost in 1 Samuel 28:18 confirms this reading.

19. See my discussion of the role that "perhaps" plays in David's story (Steussy 1999, 90–91).

20. The Hebrew verb used for Samuel's hewing in 15:33 appears nowhere else; "hewed to pieces" is a guess at meaning based on ancient translations and a later Hebrew cognate.

21. Schmidt (1994) challenges the case for ancestor consultation in ancient Israel, but cogent critiques have been brought against his own analysis; see for instance the reviews by Smith (1996) and Lewis (1999).

6. SAMUEL, HIS GOD, AND US

1. For more on fear-based religion and an alternative, see Fuller (2007).

BIBLIOGRAPHY

Abegg, Martin G., Peter W. Flint, and Eugene Charles Ulrich. 1999. *The Dead Sea Scrolls Bible: The Oldest Known Bible*. San Francisco: HarperSanFrancisco.

Alter, Robert. 1981. *The Art of Biblical Narrative*. New York: Basic Books.

———. 1999. *The David Story: A Translation with Commentary of 1 and 2 Samuel*. New York: W. W. Norton & Company.

Armstrong, Karen. 2007. *The Great Transformation: The Beginning of Our Religious Traditions*. New York: Anchor Books.

Bailey, Randall C. 1995. The Redemption of YHWH: A Literary Critical Function of the Songs of Hannah and David. *Biblical Interpretation* 3:213–31.

Barry, William A. 2008. *A Friendship Like No Other: Experiencing God's Amazing Embrace*. Chicago: Loyola Press.

Berlin, Adele. 1983. *Poetics and Interpretation of Biblical Narrative*. Sheffield, U.K.: Almond Press.

Blenkinsopp, Joseph. 1995. *Sage, Priest, Prophet: Religious and Intellectual Leadership in Ancient Israel*. Louisville, Ky.: Westminster John Knox Press.

Brueggemann, Walter. 1990. *First and Second Samuel*. Interpretation. Louisville, Ky.: John Knox Press.

———. 1992. Samuel, Book of 1–2. Pages 4:957–73 in *Anchor Bible Dictionary*. Edited by David Noel Freedman. Garden City, N.Y.: Doubleday.

Campbell, Antony F. 1975. *The Ark Narrative, 1 Sam 4–6; 2 Sam 6: A Form-Critical and Traditio-historical Study*. Society for Biblical Literature Dissertation Series 16. Missoula, Mont.: Scholars Press.

———. 1979. Yahweh and the Ark: A Case Study in Narrative. *Journal of Biblical Literature* 98:31–43.

———. 1986. *Of Prophets and Kings: A Late Ninth-Century Document (1 Samuel 1–2 Kings 10)*. Catholic Biblical Quarterly Monograph Series 17. Washington, D.C.: Catholic Biblical Association of America.

Campbell, Antony F., and Mark A. O'Brien. 2000. *Unfolding the Deuteronomistic History: Origins, Upgrades, Present Text*. Minneapolis: Fortress Press.

Clines, David J. A., and Tamara C. Eskenazi, eds. 1991. *Telling Queen Michal's Story: An Experiment in Comparative Interpretation*. Sheffield, U.K.: Sheffield Academic Press.

Coogan, Michael D., ed. 2007. *The New Oxford Annotated Bible with the Apocrypha: New Revised Standard Version*. Augm. 3rd ed. New York: Oxford University Press.

Crenshaw, James L. 1971. *Prophetic Conflict: Its Effect upon Israelite Religion*. Berlin: De Gruyter.

———. 2004. *Defending God: Biblical Responses to the Problem of Evil*. Oxford: Oxford University Press.

Cross, Frank Moore. 1973. *Canaanite Myth and Hebrew Epic: Essays in the History of the Religion of Israel*. Cambridge, Mass.: Harvard University Press.

———. 2005. *Qumran Cave 4. 12, 1–2 Samuel*. Discoveries in the Judaean Desert 17. Oxford: Clarendon Press.

Dhorme, Édouard Paul. 1910. *Les livres de Samuel*. Études Bibliques. Paris: Gabalda.

Eslinger, Lyle M. 1985. *Kingship of God in Crisis: A Close Reading of 1 Samuel 1–12*. Sheffield, U.K.: Almond Press.

Falk, Marcia. 1994. Reflections on Hannah's Prayer. *Tikkun* 9:61–64.

Fewell, Danna Nolan, and David M. Gunn. 1993. *Gender, Power, and Promise: The Subject of the Bible's First Story*. Nashville, Tenn.: Abingdon Press.

Fokkelman, J. P. 1986. *The Crossing Fates*. Vol. 2 of *Narrative Art and Poetry in the Books of Samuel*. Assen, The Netherlands: Van Gorcum.

———. 1993. *Vow and Desire*. Vol. 4 of *Narrative Art and Poetry in the Books of Samuel*. Assen, The Netherlands: Van Gorcum.

Fox, Everett. 1999. *Give Us a King! Samuel, Saul, and David*. New York: Schocken Books.

Franke, John R., and Thomas C. Oden. 2005. *Joshua, Judges, Ruth, 1–2 Samuel*. Ancient Christian Commentary on Scripture 4. Downers Grove, Ill.: InterVarsity Press.

Fuller, Robert C. 2007. Spirituality in the Flesh: The Role of Discrete Emotions in Religious Life. *Journal of the American Academy of Religion* 75:25–51.

Grizzard, Carol. 2003. Introduction and Annotations to 1 Samuel. Pages 391–477 in *The New Interpreter's Study Bible: New Revised Standard Version with Apocrypha*. Edited by Walter Harrelson. Nashville, Tenn.: Abingdon Press.

Gunn, David M. 1980. *The Fate of King Saul: An Interpretation of a Biblical Story*. Sheffield, U.K.: JSOT Press.

———. 1990. Reading Right: Reliable and Omniscient Narrator, Omniscient God, and Foolproof Composition in the Hebrew Bible. Pages 53–64 in *The Bible in Three Dimensions*. Edited by David J. A. Clines. Sheffield, U.K.: Sheffield Academic Press.

Guzik, David. N.d. David Guzik's Commentary on 1 Samuel. *Enduring Word Media*. http://www.enduringword.com/commentaries/09.htm (accessed February 5, 2009).

Halpern, Baruch. 2001. *David's Secret Demons: Messiah, Murderer, Traitor, King*. The Bible in Its World. Grand Rapids, Mich.: Eerdmans.

Hanson, Paul D. 1986. *The People Called: The Growth of Community in the Bible*. San Francisco: Harper & Row.

Harrelson, Walter J. 2003. *The New Interpreter's Study Bible: New Revised Standard Version with the Apocrypha*. Nashville, Tenn.: Abingdon Press.

Hertzberg, William. 1964. *I & II Samuel: A Commentary*. Translated by J. S. Bowden. Old Testament Library. London: SCM.

Heschel, Abraham Joshua. 1962. *The Prophets: An Introduction*. New York: Harper & Row.

Jacobsen, Thorkild. 1976. *The Treasures of Darkness: A History of Mesopotamian Religion*. New Haven, Conn.: Yale University Press.

Jameson, Fredric. 1981. *The Political Unconscious: Narrative as a Socially Symbolic Act*. Ithaca, N.Y.: Cornell University Press.

Jaspers, Karl. 1953. *The Origin and Goal of History*. Translated by Michael Bullock. New Haven, Conn.: Yale University Press.

Jobling, David. 1998. *1 Samuel*. Berit Olam: Studies in Hebrew Narrative and Poetry. A Michael Glazier Book. Collegeville, Minn.: Liturgical Press.

Jung, Carl G. 2002. *Answer to Job*. Translated by R. F. C. Hull. 50th anniversary ed. Vol. 11 of *Collected Works of C. G. Jung*. Bolingen Series 20. Princeton, N.J.: Princeton University Press.

Koch, Klaus. 1983. *The Assyrian Period*. Vol. 1 of *The Prophets*. Translated by Margaret Kohl. Philadelphia: Fortress Press.

Lewis, I. M. 1978. *Ecstatic Religion: An Anthropological Study of Spirit Possession and Shamanism*. Harmondsworth: Penguin Books.

———. 1986. *Religion in Context: Cults and Charisma*. Cambridge: Cambridge University Press.

Lewis, Theodore J. 1989. *Cults of the Dead in Ancient Israel and Ugarit*. Harvard Semitic Monographs 39. Atlanta: Scholars Press.

———. 1999. Review of Brian B. Schmidt, *Israel's Beneficent Dead: Ancestor Cult and Necromancy in Ancient Israelite Religion and Tradition*. *Journal of the American Oriental Society* 119:512–14.

McCarter, P. Kyle, Jr. 1980a. *1 Samuel: A New Translation with Introduction and Commentary*. Anchor Bible 8. Garden City, N.Y.: Doubleday.

———. 1980b. The Apology of David. *Journal of Biblical Literature* 99:489–504.

McKenzie, Steven L. 1992. Deuteronomistic History. Pages 2:160–68 in *Anchor Bible Dictionary*. Edited by David Noel Freedman. New York: Doubleday.

Meeks, Wayne A., and Jouette M. Bassler. 1993. *The HarperCollins Study Bible: New Revised Standard Version, with the Apocryphal/Deuterocanonical Books*. New York: HarperCollins.

Mettinger, Trygve N. D. 1976. *King and Messiah: The Civil and Sacral Legitimation of Israelite Kings*. Lund: CWK Gleerup.

Miller, Patrick D. 2000. *The Religion of Ancient Israel*. Library of Ancient Israel. London: SPCK.

Miscall, Peter. 1986. *1 Samuel: A Literary Reading*. Indiana Studies in Biblical Literature. Bloomington: Indiana University Press.

Moran, William L. 1963. The Ancient Near Eastern Background of the Love of God in Deuteronomy. *Catholic Biblical Quarterly* 25:77–87.

Noth, Martin. 1943. Translated and reprinted as *The Deuteronomistic History*. Journal for the Study of the Old Testament Supplement Series 15. Sheffield, U.K.: JSOT Press, 1981.

Polzin, Robert M. 1989. *Samuel and the Deuteronomist: A Literary Study of the Deuteronomic History, Pt. 2*. Indiana Studies in Biblical Literature. Bloomington: Indiana University Press.

Rad, Gerhard von. 1947. Translated and reprinted as The Deuteronomic Theology of History in I and II Kings. Pages 205–21 in *Problems of the Hexateuch and Other Essays*. Translated by E. Dicken. New York: McGraw-Hill, 1966.

Ricoeur, Paul. 1970. *Freud and Philosophy: An Essay on Interpretation*. New Haven, Conn.: Yale University Press.

Schmidt, Brian B. 1994. *Israel's Beneficent Dead: Ancestor Cult and Necromancy in Ancient Israelite Religion and Tradition*. Tübingen: J. C. B. Mohr.

Smith, Mark S. 1996. Review of Brian B. Schmidt, *Israel's Beneficent Dead: Ancestor Cult and Necromancy in Ancient Israelite Religion and Tradition*. *Catholic Biblical Quarterly* 58:724–25.

Stager, Lawrence E. 1985. The Archeology of the Family in Ancient Israel. *Bulletin of the American Schools of Oriental Research* 260:1–25.

Sternberg, Meir. 1985. *The Poetics of Biblical Narrative: Ideological Literature and the Drama of Reading*. Bloomington: Indiana University Press.

Steussy, Marti J. 1999. *David: Biblical Portraits of Power*. Studies on Personalities of the Old Testament. Columbia: University of South Carolina Press.

———. 2000. The Problematic God of Samuel. Pages 127–61 in *Shall Not the Judge of All the Earth Do What Is Right? Studies on the Nature of God in Tribute to James L. Crenshaw*. Edited by David Penchansky and Paul L. Redditt. Winona Lake, Ind.: Eisenbrauns.

———. 2002. Looking for a Friend. Paper presented at the annual meeting of the Society of Biblical Literature. Toronto, Canada, November 23–26.

———. 2004. *Psalms: Chalice Commentary for Today*. St. Louis: Chalice.

Tsumura, David Toshio. 2007. *The First Book of Samuel*. New International Commentary on the Old Testament. Grand Rapids, Mich.: Eerdmans.

Veijola, Timo. 1977. *Das Königtum in der Beurteilung der deuteronomistischen Historiographie. Eine redaktionsgeschichtliche Untersuchung*. Helsinki: Suomalainen Tiedeakatemia.

Weber, Max. 1978. *Economy and Society*. Berkeley: University of California Press.

Willis, J. T. 1971. An Anti-Elide Narrative Tradition from a Prophetic Circle at the Ramah Sanctuary. *Journal of Biblical Literature* 90:288–308.

Wilson, Robert R. 1980. *Prophecy and Society in Ancient Israel*. Philadelphia: Fortress Press.

SCRIPTURE INDEX

HEBREW WORD INDEX

All cross-references are to the topic index.

TOPIC INDEX

ABOUT THE AUTHOR

MARTI J. STEUSSY is the MacAllister-Petticrew Professor of Biblical Interpretation at Christian Theological Seminary in Indianapolis. Steussy is the author of two science fiction novels and three previous books in biblical studies, including *David: Biblical Portraits of Power.* She is also editor of the *Chalice Introduction to the Old Testament*